PRAISE FOR TOXIC CLEAN UP

Lynn Lewis-Bjostad, CMP, *President and CEO, Premier Meeting and Event Management:*

"This is a must read for all company executives. Teresa shares relatable stories and formulates a process to fix the toxic problems that plague so many workforces today. I am thrilled that someone was bold enough to address this issue. Thank you, Teresa!"

Joe Calloway, *Consultant, Speaker and Author (www.joecalloway.com) of Indispensable (Wiley & Sons), Becoming a Category of One (Wiley & Sons), and Work Like You're Showing Off (Wiley & Sons):*

"We have met the enemy, and he is us. Those words come to mind as I read Toxic Clean Up an absolute winner of a book by Teresa Day. This book should be required reading for every manager in every company no matter what the industry, product, or size of the organization. We truly are our own worst enemies in creating the very conditions at work that get in our way. This book contains hard-hitting truth, and yet is still a pleasure to read. Great work and extremely useful to today's manager."

Curt Craighead, *Owner, Best Light Communications:*

"Day's Toxic Clean Up addresses the single biggest issue suffered by American business – toxic work environments. Her understanding of the relationship between business growth and employee satisfaction creates a must-read for anyone serious about developing a productive, enjoyable and successful workplace."

TERESA DAY

TOXIC
CLEAN UP

How To Stop The Spread Of
Dysfunctional Management

Morgan James Publishing • New York

TOXIC
CLEAN UP

Library of Congress Control Number: 2007943360
ISBN: 978-1-60037-386-2 (Paperback)
ISBN: 978-1-60037-385-5 (Hardcover)

PUBLISHED BY:

Morgan James Publishing, LLC
1225 Franklin Ave Ste 325
Garden City, NY 11530-1693
Toll Free 800-485-4943
www.MorganJamesPublishing.com

MORGAN · JAMES
THE ENTREPRENEURIAL PUBLISHER ™
www.morganjamespublishing.com

Habitat
for Humanity®
Peninsula
Building Partner

GENERAL EDITOR:
Heather Campbell

COVER & INTERIOR DESIGN BY:
3 Dog Design
www.3dogdesign.net
chris@3dogdesign.net

A mind, once stretched by a new idea, never regains its original dimensions.

--Oliver Wendall Holmes

TABLE OF CONTENTS

DEDICATION

This book is for my children, Sam, Josie, Millie, Claire and Ginny. Thank you for supporting me and encouraging me throughout the whole process. You are my delight in life; may you each help make the world a better place.

And for Phil, who taught me how to let the sunlight bring the answers.

For all employees who go to work each day in a toxic pond, may you find encouragement to carry on. For those who have the ability to bring about positive change in the work environment, may you find the inspiration to do so.

INTRODUCTION

Ponds & Frogs: What They Tell Us

As the gentle breeze touches the surface of the water and slight ripples edge across the pond like endless marching rows of soldiers, the pond looks, well, normal. A thick stand of rushes line the north edge, interspersed with alligator weed. A long-ago fallen log sits halfway in the water, halfway out, like a fashion runway extending into the crowd on which the geese take their daily turn. A fish or two zips up close to the surface, turning tail and swimming deep again. A turtle even sticks his head out to look at you, wondering what you are doing in his yard. Still, something is missing. You can't quite put your finger on it, but you know everything isn't right with this pond.

The crickets chirp and the locusts buzz, and then suddenly you know what's missing. "Why aren't the frogs croaking?" you wonder, and start to look around for the familiar creatures, glimpsing only one or two hopping around. Ponds and frogs—like peanut butter and jelly, like a horse and carriage, like Easter and eggs—how is it possible to have one without the other? But, today, you can't find many frogs. Puzzled, you keep looking. And looking. And looking. What has happened to all of the frogs?

FROGS INDICATE OVERALL POND HEALTH

Frogs are very sensitive creatures, absorbing both water and oxygen through their skin. Frogs also occupy two levels on the food chain, a lower level as the less complex larvae and tadpole, and a higher level as the mature frog. That's why scientists often use them as indicators of the overall health of the pond environment. They also live in both the aquatic and land ecosystems. They have a lot of exposure to the elements in many different ways, and thus their overall health indicates many things about the environment on many different levels.

Sometimes, adverse pond conditions themselves cannot be identified, but their effects can be seen in the frogs. For scientists measuring environmental health, it basically comes down to this: *If the frogs are sick, the pond is toxic.*

The same can be said of the workplace environment. When toxic management practices are present through-out the organization, the employees are the ones who are affected. As a group, they have the most exposure to all of the elements of the organization—its culture, managerial practices, and people. The employees carry out the daily tactical actions of the company, each department complet-ing the tasks that, in the end, make the company work as an organization. The overall "health" of the employees indi-cates the overall health of the workplace, as surely as the frogs indicate the health of the pond.

TOXIC FACTORS COMBINE WITH NATURAL CAUSES

Pollution, pesticides and other toxins interfere with nature's regular cycle of life. Disease has always been a built-in natural control for all animal populations. But with toxic interference, the natural process of death may become an epidemic, wiping out entire populations. If you cannot find many frogs in the pond, you can be sure that toxic influ-ences have damaged them and their habitat.

Interestingly, scientists often cannot point to one *specific* factor that creates a toxic pond. Instead, it's a complex for-mula of many causes. Climate changes, disease, pesticides, and pollution combine to create an environment that is just plain unhealthy.

The same is true in the work environment. Rarely is there only one factor at work in a dysfunctional environment. *One* negative factor can be rather easily identified and eliminated. An ineffective boss can be replaced. A poor process can be improved. But when the attitudes and behaviors of the organization, and in management in particular, are entrenched in dysfunction, identifying root causes in order to improve the entire environment can be challenging. The frogs cannot thrive in a toxic pond, and neither can your employees.

In the following chapters, we'll take a look at the root causes of a toxic work environment and what you can do to clean it up. We'll also discuss the two foundational elements that must be in place for robust workplace health, and create a plan for keeping your "pond" healthy and productive.

x

PART 1

The Seven Deadly Toxins

Deadly Toxin 1: Stifling Talent

Work while you have the light. You are responsible for the talent that has been entrusted to you.

--Henri Frederic Amiel

The group filed into the meeting room silently. One by one, they filled the chairs around the large oval conference table. A couple of quick nods, a short "morning" to a late-comer, and the silence just sat there with all ten of them, waiting for Bob Wallers to come in and start the meeting. All ten were dreading the morning; this meeting should be a strategic sit-down to figure out why sales were spiraling downward on the Web site of this Fortune 50 retailer. Instead, it was going to be a grueling tongue-lashing by Wallers, the division head of Internet Marketing. In this room, the facts didn't matter.

The people around the table represented several departments and functions: IT programmers, web content designers, a creative director, a finance person, a copywriter and two department managers. The room held a good deal of talent and thoughtfulness. On their own, the team had plenty of opinions as to why this segment of the Web retail site was floundering, and they were mostly centered around Waller's decision months ago to modify the navigation of the site.

His objective was to "clean up" the landing pages, but as a result of removing quite a number of links and categories, the shoppers had to get through several more pages before they could buy the product. In some cases, they might not even be able to easily find the product, it was buried so deep in the new navigation scheme. Sales had fallen off substantially, but Bob was looking for answers outside his own decisions. He didn't want to hear about the navigation.

To break the silence, David, one of the department managers asked "Is anybody going to be brave enough to bring up the navigation changes as the reason for declining sales?"

There was nervous laughter and the creative director said, "Are you?"

"I'm actually thinking about it...." trailed off David as Wallers marched into the room, closing the door behind him. He sat down heavily in his chair at the head of the table and opened a manila folder in front of him.

"Good morning, Team," he said as he glanced around the room, taking in all the participants and their respective roles. "What are the conclusions?"

Wallers drummed his fingers on the table. Before anyone could answer, Wallers spoke again, "Ken, did you get the report as to whether the buyers were selling different merch in the stores than they were on the site?"

"Yes, I did, and it's basically 100% the same merchandise," said Ken, wincing a little as if anticipating a blow.

David had decided earlier that there was simply no winning the situation so he might as well take the plunge and say what everyone was thinking. "Bob, the only likely culprit is the navigation. Is there any way we can delay launching the remaining segments of the site until we can thoroughly examine and test this segment? We run the risk of sales declining in additional segments if we launch next month as planned for the rest of the site."

Wallers drew in a deep breath, and narrowing his eyes as he turned toward David, and slowly exhaled. He started speaking, but more slowly than normal, as if someone had turned down the speed on a tape, "We...have been...over this...a hundred....times." He was speeding up now, back to normal pace, "Why are you bringing that up again?" Wallers actually stood up at his chair, placing his large hands on the table and leaning forward, splaying out his fingers. The volume of his voice was increasing, "Look, here's the situation. If we launch in March, I get all of my bonus. If we launch in May, I get 80%. If we launch in July, I get 50%." Now he was shouting. "When the hell do you think we are going to launch?" and he glared one last time around the room and left.

TELLTALE TOXIC SIGNS

David and the other employees in this room are feeling the poisonous effects of the Toxin of Stifling Talent. This retail business is attempting to unravel a problem and find the source so that it can be corrected. The staff that assembled to discuss the problem is talented, smart, intuitive, and educated about the issues surrounding the problem. Given the task to complete on their own, they likely would have come up with a good plan suggesting answers. But Bob Wallers wasn't interested in answers that didn't support his personal agenda, which was to achieve his bonus level regardless of business issues anybody else was worried about.

His overbearing and restrictive manner stifles any real talent that can be applied to the situation. Afraid to risk their jobs, the team couldn't get to the heart of the problem as they saw it because Wallers wouldn't allow it.

TRADING DOLLARS FOR CONTRIBUTION

David is a dedicated employee who is slowly becoming ill swimming in a toxic pond. But he is not alone in his workplace troubles. In another company pond, another talented employee is being slowly poisoned by the same toxin.

Nancy Hughes is the Senior Director of Event Planning at a large home decor manufacturing and sales company. Prior to a Senior Management change, Nancy had reported to a boss who encouraged her to use all of her skill set, and recognized her for her work. Nancy felt empowered to do an even better job, and worked tirelessly in order to prove to her boss that her faith in her was not misplaced.

She loved coming to work and described it to her friends and family as "having a place at the table" which meant to her that her opinion mattered, and that she contributed to the overall success of the company by leading her team's efforts.

Nancy was well known in the meeting planning industry. She would receive at least one call a month from a recruiter or another company seeking to hire her, but she was simply not interested. She gained such satisfaction from her work, and felt such a part of a productive team, that she never even returned the calls.

Then a management change came about. Nancy had a new boss, and a new CEO. She did not know what to expect, and was thrilled to receive a promotion and a substantial raise. But over the next six months, she became increasingly disappointed in her new circumstances. She felt completely pushed aside--her opinion was no longer consulted or needed, event plans and schedules were made without her input, and the new boss took over many of the decisions she was previously responsible for.

Despite the raise and promotion, Nancy started looking elsewhere. "I'd give back both the raise and the promotion to have my 'seat at the table' again," she'd say.

And next time the phone rings, Nancy will likely return the call.

Recruiting phone calls and employment offers come to good employees. They just do. It's important to note that when Nancy had lower pay and title but more empowerment to exercise her talents, she was happy and productive.

People will trade dollars and prestige for a chance to build something meaningful and contribute to the overall goals of the company. Yes, the paycheck matters; but employees are also looking to satisfy needs for achievement, recognition, and personal growth. Individuals feel responsible to employ their talents; that is, to make use of them. When talented employees are stifled by overbearing management or lack of opportunity, they will become increasingly unhappy in their roles.

MAN VS. MACHINE

Fredrick Winslow Taylor (1856-1915) was one of the first individuals to analyze human behavior in the workplace, and put together a system that could manage the larger numbers of employees and materials that the Industrial Revolution had brought together. He created the model of "scientific management," and thus began the still on-going fascination of studying employees, managers and environments in the workplace.

Fredrick Taylor modeled his ideas after a machine itself, with each person having a responsibility, like each part in a machine. But he took the idea even further: just as the machine should have cheap, interchangeable and passive parts, so too should the worker be cheap to hire, be interchangeable with others, and play a passive role in the overall organization.

Fredrick's goal was to reduce any variables that the humanity of the workforce could introduce, and focus on speed, cost, capacity and production. Though we are long past the Industrial Revolution, Fredrick's ideas have a strong hold on the American business psyche even today.

WHERE FREDRICK WENT WRONG

The value of a job is often thought of as simply what has to be paid to an individual in order to get that task accomplished. Employers typically want to pay the lowest possible amount to secure the most qualified individual for the task. And often "not enough pay" is a reason people leave a current position in search of a better one. It's simple economics: there are bills to pay, and the job has to supply enough money to meet those needs.

But should the economic factor be the single definition of the value of a job? Hardly. And in today's economy and with the strong push for flexible hours, job sharing, telecommuting and other employee-focused initiatives, it better not be.

Every employee at any level would prefer a workplace that allows them to experience feelings of contribution and achievement. Just because every person who needs to work might not have the luxury of seeking out that kind of workplace, you as a leader and employer should pay close attention to creating opportunities in your pond.

When the economy is growing strong and competition is high for dedicated employees, the workplaces that follow Fredrick's model of assuming that pay alone is the primary motivator for workers will continually lose out on the best people.

Whether or not this model worked for the Industrial Revolution, it certainly won't work in today's climate. Employers must focus on what Fredrick tried to ignore: the variables of humanity; those affectations, habits, and abilities that set us apart from one another. In a word, Talent.

WHAT IS TALENT, ANYWAY?

Talent--hard to define, but you know it when you see it, right? Fredrick wanted to assume that two individuals who perform similar job functions could be seen as interchangeable, just like parts in a machine. So when one employee leaves, another one simply steps up to do the job. While this approach to management might (barely) work in assembly line production facilities, it is severely limited for application anywhere else.

Yet still, many company leaders and managers follow this philosophy. Some even consider it a particularly fine opportunity to display their power to say about a disgruntled employee, "Well then, fire that person and go find someone who will do it" as if you could walk to the employee parts store and purchase a replacement.

Ego-driven CEOs and upper managers also add their own peculiar twist to this notion. Not only is everyone inter-changeable, but somehow they also believe "if I just had enough time, I could do your job better than you. I only hire you and pay you to do it because my time is filled up with being CEO, or (insert any title)."

But Fredrick, and these leaders, are wrong. People are not machines, they are individual bundles of energy, motiva-tion, compassion, and desire for achievement. They are a mix of every experience of their upbringing and education, of their interactions and gene pool. And when a talented worker walks out of your building, whether she is a telephone opera-tor in the Call Center, an accountant in the Finance depart-ment, or the Senior Vice President of Sales, she walks out with much, much more than a job description.

Take the Call Center phone operator for example. Her name is Cecilia, and she had the most amazing flair for calm-ing down the most irate of customers. Some combination of the quality of her voice--soothing and gentle, along with her vocabulary and southern accent, "Now honey, I know, I know...." immediately diffused situations that other opera-tors couldn't handle. Sympathy and compassion for the call-er's point of view just flowed out of her. But the real talent came in her ability to soothe the customer and convince them at the same time that while she understood their issue, the solution may not be exactly what they wanted. Cecilia had a stellar satisfaction rating among both her callers and her colleagues for customer-centered problem solving that kept the company's objectives intact.

Replacing Cecilia means far more than finding another person who can answer the phone. Therefore, keeping Cecilia should be one of her manager's priorities.

All employees want to perform work that is interesting and challenging, and in the performance of the work, be recognized for their contribution. As they continue to contribute and continue to be rewarded and recognized, they hope to be promoted or challenged at another level, to continue improvement and moving forward. They want to be supported by their bosses, believed in by management, and respected by their peers. Which of these components is more meaningful to the employee is a completely individual choice, and not even really necessary to understand--as long as the company is putting in place an environment that feeds this cycle.

Both David and Nancy were performing work that was interesting to them. But the toxin of Stifling their Talent was driving both of them to seek shelter in another pond, when they otherwise wouldn't leave. They were both kept from exercising their talents by poor choices and decisions by their management teams.

Over time, the Toxin of Stifling Talent leaves you with a workforce comprised of people who can't leave due to obligations, or those who can disconnect from their jobs and perform by rote. Either way, your pond will become sicker and sicker. Workers who are disengaged from their jobs are absent more frequently, don't work as hard while at the job, and can cost the company millions of dollars in lost opportunities. It will always cost you more to replace a good employee, even if you pay the newcomer a lesser wage, because of the institutional knowledge and experience they take with them.

Jack Milling had a reputation with two sides: he had a genius IQ, had been with the company for over 30 years, and knew everything and everybody. He was the gatekeeper of the company's history and heritage, and no communication could leave the building without being passed by his eagle eye, both for proofreading, and for accuracy. But he was also hard to get along with, his desk was always a clutter closet, embarrassingly so, and if he didn't get his way, he'd often pout like a child.

New management decided they didn't need to put up with that, and as they let him go, they asked him to write down everything he knew so that the next person could pick up where he left off. That is, quite frankly, a ridiculous request. In making the decision that his attitude was something they wanted to lose, they also decided his institutional knowledge would go with him.

Intuition, knowledge, experience, personal warmth and energy--those thing which make us individuals--can never be transferred to another as if they were a binary language of 0s and 1s, like computer code.

Additionally, employers who ignore this Toxin of Stifling Talent run the risk that these workers will go to work for the competition, who has built a better workplace environment, and encourages contribution and achievement.

Many studies have been done on the replacement costs of a high-level employee, and they range from 75 percent of the departing employee's salary to the recent Ernst & Young survey calculation of 150 percent. These calculations typically include new hiring costs, training costs, the cost of lost productivity, etc. But they don't take into account the hundreds of ways the talented individual's departure may ripple through the organization. How can you measure the enthusiasm for the day's work that the talented individual instilled in his co-workers that has now disappeared? How can you measure the degree to which other employees aspired to develop similar qualities in themselves, and have now lost their role model?

You can't take these things into account because they can't be measured. But their loss can easily be reflected in your bottom line without you even realizing it.

BABY, BABY

And it gets worse: the Baby Boomers are retiring and the new generation of employees see the world through completely different sunglasses--hip and personalized. Generation Xers demand what Baby Boomers saw as privilege: freedom, flexibility, and recognition. And they are much less willing to put up with what they see as nonsense than the workers they are replacing.

Lynn Franco is the Director of The Conference Board's Consumer Research Center, and conducts surveys on work attitudes. She said recently, "Rapid technological changes, rising productivity demands and changing employee expectations have all contributed to the decline in job satisfaction. As large numbers of baby boomers prepare to leave the workforce, they will be increasingly replaced by younger workers, who ... have different attitudes and expectations about the role of work in their lives. This transition will present a new challenge for employers."

CRITICISM KILLS

When talented employees begin to question whether their own contribution to the organization is appreciated or useful, it is most likely because they are trying to function in an overly critical environment. Criticism stifles talent and creates self-doubt in individuals who have been successful for years prior to working in this particular toxic environment.

A former consultant with a Big Five firm and very successful Public Relations professional, Carol Demming accepted an offer from a client as their PR Specialist. She had been happy working as a consultant, but was excited about putting down some long-term roots instead of handing off her projects to be maintained by someone else.

Carol was also very excited about this particular company and its work empowering women to start their own businesses. Carol got to work right away doing what she does best, and in 6 months took the company from zero "impressions" to hundreds of mentions in major newspapers, radio spots, features, and magazines. She also brought the company's Charitable Foundation into the spotlight, raising money and awareness.

But the pond Carol had joined was toxic, and she was being slowly poisoned by the Toxin of Stifling Talent. Even though the senior management team had hired her to do a very specific job, and she was in fact meeting those expectations, they didn't really see value in what she was accomplishing. She loved working for her direct boss, the Vice President of Marketing, but was constantly bombarded by questions about her choices from his boss, the Senior Vice President of Sales & Marketing, who often dealt directly with Carol, bypassing the chain of command all together. Even though Carol consistently performed to her own boss' expectations, the SVP constantly criticized her for her action or inaction, or ignored her and made public relations decisions without her input.

After 12 months in this toxic pond, Carol began to wonder what it was she was good at and couldn't remember why she took this position. Formerly a bright shining star at a very competitive company, the poisons had done their work on her. She said, "I know I'm good at this. I have client referrals and awards. I received commended status on all my projects. But somehow, since I've been at this company, I am questioning what I know is true about my abilities."

The Toxin had done its dirty work.

WHY IT MATTERS

David, Nancy, Cecilia, Jack, and Carol are all real people working for real employers. But beware: The Toxin of Stifling Talent is not something that happens at other companies. It's likely happening in your company, and it's up to you as an owner or leader to make sure it isn't killing your talented employees. The only sure way to do that is rid yourself of the Toxin of Stifling Talent, and educate your management team to do the same.

Employee turnover is expensive. Your company may spend thousands of dollars annually finding the best employees, recruiting them, training them, possibly even relocating them. Why would you not follow through and make sure once they arrive that they'll want to stay?

Keeping your employees once you've hired them will make you more productive, more profitable, enable you to keep your customers longer, and increase their satisfaction with your product or service. Who doesn't want that?

TO LEARN HOW TO REMOVE DEADLY TOXIN 1: STIFLING TALENT FROM YOUR WORKPLACE, READ CLEAN UP 1: COMMIT TO THE PROCESS.

Deadly Toxin 1 Poison Control:
Are you stifling talent?
Your particular circumstances may not resemble the ones discussed here, but surely there are ways to improve your pond. Answer these two questions to explore ways your pond may be toxic. If you are very brave, have your staff answer them as well!

1. What part of my management style/management requirements is telling my employees that I don't trust them to do a good job without my help and intervention?

2. What measures can I take in my area at work to ensure my most talented employees are empowered to exercise those talents?

Deadly Toxin 2: The Blame Game

*Nearly all men can stand adversity, but
if you want to test a man's character,
give him power.*

--Abraham Lincoln

Aaron Hay took a slow sip of coffee, holding the cup to his lips and staring out his window at the parking lot to the side of the building. He was unraveling a puzzle in his mind, and did not like the conclusion he was reaching. A dedicated professional, Aaron took pride in his work and his abilities, not just as CIO in a large manufacturing and sales company, but as a businessman who could contribute to the overall company plan. Today, he was pretty sure he didn't want to be here anymore.

He put the coffee cup down on his desk and sighed. It was time to address the team. He left his office for the small conference room around the corner, where his staff of developers and designers had assembled for this meeting. They looked grim, worried as much about him as they were about themselves.

"Well," began Aaron, "as you know, I met with the CEO yesterday about his desire to move up the deadline for this project." Aaron paused. "He impressed upon me the necessity of launching 45 days earlier than we had planned, and as it stands, we need to back up that launch. I'll be reworking your assignments and we'll meet again this afternoon to distribute the load. Thanks."

The team shuffled out of the room, each one looking at Aaron at they exited. They trusted their boss, and they knew that he was protecting them from the harsh reality of what really happened. They all surmised back at their cubes that the conversation had gone something more like this:

Aaron: *I can't execute to this timeline and also include appropriate time for testing.*

The CEO: *There is no other choice; it must be done. I'm sure you'll do a fine job.*

Aaron: *I understand your wish for expediency, but this is complicated code and the way our systems are designed, the complexity you want added will take….*

The CEO: *I'm sure you will get it done. That's all.*

The team was mostly correct in their assumptions about the conversation, though they added a few more colorful words. Aaron had been in front of the CEO for the past four months with the open items, trying to get decisions nailed down so the team could progress. His efforts proved unproductive, as the CEO couldn't decide through some of the major obstacles. Finally, he worked through the issues, providing answers for the open items. But by this time, the project was already derailed from its original timeline. And now he wanted the entire project launched 45 days early, in hopes to squash some customer dissatisfaction that had arisen over the company's systems.

Aaron was afraid of just the opposite. The unforgiving timeline gave him just enough room to get the project launched, but not enough to adequately test it to remove all the bugs. Customer dissatisfaction had the potential to reach an all-time high. And Aaron knew, should that happen, he would be on the line, not the CEO.

The same thing had happened one time before, but on a smaller scale. The CEO had made an unreasonable demand at the end of the month for a reporting tool he wanted built for the sales force. Aaron worked with him on the specifications, then let him know that the best timeline would be to launch the tool in two phases, giving the team time to refine the second part, which was more complicated and could produce more errors if not well-tested. The CEO said hotly, "Aaron, can you do the job or not? If you can't, I'm sure there are guys waiting out there who can. Now, what'll it be?"

Aaron acquiesced, and the team scrambled to get it done. They squeaked through with minimal errors, but as luck would have it, one of the head salesmen tried out the tool and reported a major bug directly back to the CEO. Aaron's team was soundly whip lashed for committing to the project to begin with. "You know I rely on you to tell me if your resources can handle this sort of operation," the CEO thundered during the monthly staff meeting. "Aaron, get it right next time!"

This was the puzzle Aaron was attempting to solve. He finally understood that it didn't matter whether or not the team could reasonably perform the necessary work. The only thing that mattered was that the CEO was going to get his way, and if things went south, it would never be his fault or responsibility. Though he felt badly about abandoning his team, Aaron knew he had to start looking for work somewhere else if wanted to keep his own sanity.

TELLTALE TOXIC SIGNS

Aaron and his team are feeling the poisonous effects from the Toxin of The Blame Game. In this case, the leadership created a situation in which success was impossible, required assent and execution by the team, then blamed the team when it failed to meet expectations. Leaders who spread the Toxin of The Blame Game avoid taking responsibility for failure at nearly any cost. These leaders have even been known to twist circumstances and conversations to sidestep any culpability. The project might have failed, but by golly, *they* didn't fail. Unfortunately, the toxin won't stop there, because the Toxin of The Blame Game needs someone to be responsible, as long as its someone *else*.

The Toxin of the Blame Game leads to demotivation, resentment, and lower productivity in the team, as the executive feeds his ego and does not accept responsibility for his own decisions. It also leads to the most talented workers abandoning the pond.

The Toxin of the Blame Game can thrive in any size organization—it doesn't matter how many employees are present, or how much revenue is produced, how many computers it owns, or the size of the building. Frequently, the Toxin of the Blame Game spreads when the leader's ego is threatened.

DESTRUCTIVE LEADERSHIP

Individuals reach high leadership levels for a variety of reasons, talent to do the job being one of the least frequent. Graduating #1 in the class from Harvard Business School might make someone intelligent, or a good student; it doesn't necessarily make them wise, or any sort of a good leader. In fact, individuals are often promoted on their solo performance—stellar sales, great design, or a hundred other factors that have nothing to do with the ability to lead a group of people and make progress toward a common goal.

Entrepreneurs with vision often make the worst CEO's for the very reasons that turned their ideas into a company to start with: drive, ambition, and perfectionism. Coupled with ego and insecurity, the combination of power without emotional competence can be deadly poison to the environment. Being in charge also gives them a stable of people who can be blamed for failure, should the need arise to defend their actions.

Because of this dysfunctional leadership, the staff's energy goes into jockeying for position, office politics, worrying about the job or pay, or potential lay offs. Each of these is a major distraction to producing quality work to advance the company's goals.

The Deadly Toxin of The Blame Game takes its most poisonous form when the executive feels that when things go wrong, the employee who caused the wrong must be punished. This leader does not focus on *what* went wrong and how to fix it so that it doesn't happen again, but rather on *who did* wrong, and what punishment is suitable. This leader needs a target, and an outlet. This is a rather strange and ineffective way to run a business, as it treats employees as wayward children who need to be corrected. Employees are decidedly *not* wayward children, but grown adults, engaged in an employment "agreement" with their company: "I will perform such and such work, and you will pay me such and such wage."

Nowhere in present-day America is any boss entitled to "punish" an employee who makes a mistake. This is not part of the agreement between an employer and an employee; it is, however, an unfortunate part of humanity—one of the worst parts of it, since it services ego and insecurity. This attitude assumes employees show up to work each day apathetic at best, and at worst, intent on destroying both their future and the company. This is generally not part of any worker's plan for their day.

True professionals who are good at their jobs and take their work seriously are not above taking responsibility for any action that fails. But making a mistake at work does not constitute a character flaw, which is the way these professionals are often made to feel.

Ego and insecurity can also prohibit leaders from recognizing the talent levels of their staff. These leaders can only see as far as their own limited sight can project, and in their arrogance of belief that they are the smartest person they know, they cannot extend any credit to anyone who might be more talented than themselves. They cannot recognize it because it is too threatening. As a result, the business will only grow to be the size of their own limitations.

Wayne Hochwarter, Management Professor at Florida State University, surveyed over 700 people from different industries with questions about their supervisors. The results, published in the Fall 2007 edition of *Leadership Quarterly*, report that 23% of the respondents have experience with a supervisor who blames others to cover up mistakes or to minimize embarrassment. And 31% of respondents had been given the "silent treatment" by their supervisor in the past year. The silent treatment? Is this third grade? No, unfortunately, it is not third grade. It is the environment that nearly a third of all employees suffer through when their leaders are not emotionally equipped to be in charge, and give into the need to make someone around them uncomfortable.

THE ROLE OF FEAR

Fear is a very strong motivator, no doubt. But it is the wrong kind of motivator when the goal is to organize a group of people to work for a common vision and the meeting of a set of objectives. Fear overrides productivity, reverses it, and squashes all the connectedness that is possible when a group of people come together to work. Creative problem solving necessarily involves taking risks, but if the team is afraid of losing their jobs or being ridiculed for their ideas, they will only play in the ultra-safe zone, which limits their creative power and insight.

Some leaders feel they must enforce their own will onto their employees by at least the threat of some awful thing happening. They don't trust their staff to make the right decisions, or produce the appropriate quality of work without some peril attached to failure. No manager will get stellar results from a threatened team. This approach only produces a poor outcome. Even if the results turn out okay, the emotional passion and energy the team could have ignited to produce a great outcome will never get lit. In fact, everyone will work very hard to stay under the radar, doing nothing to call special attention to themselves.

There is not an employee or CEO working today in any company who has not made a mistake. Many, many mistakes, most likely. Anyone who is passionate about the job and reaches for creative solutions will eventually make a mistake. But a mistake is generally not a death knell, though these leaders treat it as such. Mistakes at work should be learning opportunities to better processes or to address issues. If an employee needs to be corrected, then it should be done with respect and in private.

Unfortunately, many managers and leaders take the liberty of correcting and finding fault with employees at staff meetings or other public venues, in order "to make an example" of him, and presumably to motivate everyone else to avoid the same fate. This could be called Management by Intimidation. Blaming employees in public is a sure sign the Toxin of The Blame Game is spreading throughout the pond, ultimately discouraging communication, demoralizing employees, and driving the best talent to another pond with a healthier environment.

LACK OF TRUST

When the leadership yells, berates, and belittles as their management style, a decided lack of trust develops on the part of the employee. If the leader ever does offer a word of praise, it is met with suspicion. The employee may wonder, *"Why are you complimenting me? Have I done something wrong?"* This is an obvious contradiction, but it makes more sense to the employee than a boss who blames one day and compliments the next.

Leaders sometimes forget that trust is a foundational component of their business, both between them and their customers, and between them and their employees. The leaders' failure to make trust a priority will mean they won't safeguard it and prevent it from being destroyed.

Another surprising result in the Hochwarter survey had to do with leaders who steal credit, or fail to give credit, for ideas or work from their employees. Stealing credit also builds a huge lack of trust, on a team or within a manager/employee relationship.

Credibility is like a bank account—there's a certain balance in there, and continual withdrawals will knock the balance down to zero. When it's gone, it's pretty much gone forever.

Sometimes being in charge is a charge all its own, and managers resort to fueling their egos or other dysfunctional feelings by bullying or *mis*-managing their employees by making them feel vulnerable.

Trust cannot exist in a blaming environment. But without trust in the workplace between managers and employees, resentment and suspicion grow, and the progress of the business shrinks. For some people, blaming is so much easier than constructive collaborative problem solving. Blaming covers up fear, inadequacy, and inability.

THE EROSION OF PROFESSIONAL BOUNDARIES

Professional boundaries are those stopping points all employees know and understand about their jobs and responsibilities. In a good environment, clarity surrounding these boundaries is a part of the culture; in a toxic one, the boundary lines continually shift, and are never quite clear. This is the way a toxic boss wants it. She wants to shift responsibilities according to what mood she's in or what project is at hand.

Boundaries are a good thing in the workplace—frustration stays low because people know what they are responsible for, and maybe more importantly, what they are NOT responsible for. Work can be accomplished efficiently, targets defined and hit. All is well.

Some flexibility among teams is a good thing, but when boundaries are poorly defined, work gets repeated and no one is accountable for appropriate results. The employee who might be held accountable might never have had the appropriate clarity around the project…the blaming begins and never ends until the Toxin is removed from the pond.

In the toxic environment of The Blame Game, the leader won't want boundaries because they make accountabilities clear, thus negating the need for blame, or the opportunity for blame. These dysfunctional leaders are creating a workplace environment that mirrors their personal environments, because that is where they are most comfortable.

The toxic leader also won't want employees with good interpersonal boundaries, because she will require their time as if it were her own. This toxin tends to be spread by leaders with particularly poor boundaries of their own, and they often don't see where they end and others begin—and the expectation is that the employee will be just as excited about working all weekend as they are—or at least feel the obligation to do it!

Then there are those who don't work all weekend, but require their employees to do it, almost as if on their behalf. It's easy to get pulled into the trap as well. Accolades and compliments, maybe even a pay raise and a promotion for all that hard work, lands you in a place you ultimately don't want to be—roped to the office or Blackberry.

It doesn't feel right for many employees to set their own boundaries--to push back, to say no, or to keep other commitments. This makes them an easy target for blame, for one. Plus, it feels like betrayal, especially if others are pulling the load. It can cause hurt feelings and resentment, especially if the boundaries are undefined and a workaholic boss is setting them for the employees.

THE BLAME GAME USUALLY INVOLVES HEARING LOSS

A manager caught in the toxicity of The Blame Game will generally not be able to hear you when you try to set appropriate boundaries or discuss reasonable timelines. Everything must make sense to the already established line of reasoning set up by the leader who must be allowed to blame others for their failures.

Kay worked as a Vice President in a refreshment services company, but her boss, the senior executive in charge of Sales and Communications insisted on being involved in every detail of every decision, even to the point of reviewing the communication releases that Kay's staff prepared. Kay is a very capable executive, and had come to realize over her 14 months in the job that she was merely an appendage in this organization. What the senior executive really wanted was a working staff to execute her own ideas, not a high-level planner and visionary thinker. Kay decided it was time to move on to another workplace. After she had received an offer, she met with her boss to discuss her resignation. Kay thought if she could explain the situation clearly, it might help the next person who came to work here. But the senior executive simply could not "hear" what she was saying.

Kay began, "I am resigning because in your management style, you really prefer to be very involved with the staff-level employees to execute your vision. You simply don't need me to operate at my level of strategic input and planning."

The senior executive replied, "You know, I really understand. There's a lot going on here, and it's hard to juggle all of the projects at once."

Surprised, Kay said, "Um, that's not it at all. In fact, I am very good at multi-tasking and juggling a lot of work. The issue is that I can't work under your management style."

The senior executive replied, "You know, I really understand. You came from a completely different environment. We do things differently around here, and it's been hard for you to adjust."

Now astonished at her inability to hear the truth, Kay said, "Really that's not it at all. In your management style, you prefer to work directly with the staff that is executing the request, even to the level of making edits on press releases. There really isn't room for me to use my skill set in strategic planning and project management in this environment."

The senior executive was becoming noticeably flustered. In a more strident voice, she continued, "I understand. You didn't really know what you were getting into when you came here. It's probably best that you move on to an environment you are better suited for."

Kay finally gave up, ending the exit interview by saying, "We just don't see the situation the same way. Thank you for the opportunity."

The senior executive had to mold the situation into something she could be comfortable with. Kay realized she couldn't make a difference in this pond and moved on.

WHY IT MATTERS

So what happens when talented employees work for blame game leaders? Ultimately, the town ain't big enough for the two of them; and unfortunately for the business, it is usually the talent that leaves.

Blamers blame for many reasons, none of which move the business forward in a sensible fashion. They blame to keep the attention off their own short-comings or inability to solve a particular problem. They blame to shift the focus on to an employee if someone in the organization is unhappy with them. Occasionally, The Blame Game turns nastier if the blamer develops into a bully at the workplace.

When employees leave for another job, they often don't express their true concerns to their managers or to Human Resources. It's just easier to take the path of least resistance, say everything is great and exit quietly. Plus, they may feel their livelihood is at risk, should a new employer call to ask the question, "Is this individual available for re-hire?" Deciding the battle is no longer worth fighting, the talent flees the pond, and the business suffers.

TO LEARN HOW TO REMOVE DEADLY TOXIN 2: THE BLAME GAME, FROM YOUR WORKPLACE, READ CLEAN UP 2: CELEBRATE AND GIVE CREDIT.

Deadly Toxin 2 Poison Control:
Are you playing the blame game?
Your particular circumstances may not resemble the ones discussed here, but surely there are ways to improve your pond. Answer these two questions to explore ways your pond may be toxic. If you are very brave, have your staff answer them as well!

1. Can you identify a situation in your workplace where the Toxin of The Blame Game was at work? Were you involved in the situation? How could it have been resolved differently?

2. List out the effects the Blame Game has had on your staff and your projects at your workplace.

Deadly Toxin 3: Ignoring Burn Out

We must learn our limits. We are all something, but none of us are everything.

--Blaise Pascal

"Where the devil is Nick?" Carmen said out loud as she called his cell phone for the fourth time. She was waiting on him to bring some materials from the office over to the sales event he was in charge of, and she was getting nervous as the beginning time was fast approaching.

Finally he answered. "Nick! Where in the world are you??"

"You don't know?" he replied with surprise.

"Know what?" she asked a little panicky.

"I got laid off about an hour ago," he said. "They didn't tell you?"

Carmen felt sick. This was Nick's event! She wasn't even supposed to be here, she only volunteered to come set up at the last minute because everyone on the team was already so overwhelmed. She didn't even know the contact's name at the hotel! "Call Kelly," said Nick, naming their direct supervisor. "She'll know what to do."

As the phone rang in Kelly's office, Kelly sat at her desk staring at her computer. Her boss had dropped in earlier to tell her that one of her staff had been cut and that the group admin for sales had also been cut. Already understaffed for the workload in her department, she couldn't even begin to formulate the plan to absorb the work that these two employees performed. In fact, since she was not told beforehand of the planned lay off, she didn't even know the exact status of their projects, as their weekly status meeting update wasn't until tomorrow.

She finally picked up the phone. "This is Kelly. Oh, hi Carmen. Yeah, that's something, isn't it? No, I didn't know it was coming. The box of materials? Yes, I'll send someone over with it right away. The hotel contact is Cheryl Smith, and I'll send Doug over there soon to help you. Okay, thanks." She hung up the phone, wondering how she was going to juggle the project she had to pull Doug from to manage this crisis.

Her doctor had recently told her that the stress of working nights and weekends was causing her blood pressure to go through the roof, and if she kept ignoring it, she'd cause long-term damage to her health. She knew he was right and had started making a plan that included more balance in her life between work and non-work. It was hardly apparent any more where the lines ended and began.

But now! She knew she'd be expected to pick up the slack. There was a company meeting in an hour where she'd get a nice pep talk about everybody doing their share to shoulder the remaining work. She could hardly stomach attending.

Her company, a Northern textiles company, overconfident after two great top line revenue years, expanded quickly, implementing a new compensation structure for its sales force and beginning new programs for employees. But the company was struggling as sales dipped, then declined, as Toxin 1 and 2 were at work spreading poison. This morning was the third lay off in 18 months, and came as a complete shock to everyone since in order to quell any leaks only a few people on the senior management team even knew it was coming. Employees came to work and were sent home, managers came to work and were informed their staff had been cut.

The CEO called a brief meeting in the lunchroom for the stunned employees. He told them that they'd all have to pull a little harder since there were now fewer rowers, but he believed in them to get the job done.

TELLTALE TOXIC SIGNS

Carmen and Kelly are feeling the poisonous effects of the Toxin of Ignoring Burnout. Already overloaded with a heavy work schedule divided among too few staff members, they now feel helpless to get their own work done, and support the company's goals effectively. The leaders of the company have made it clear that there is no alternative; the existing employees must shoulder the load and continue to meet expectations. It is a particular kind of arrogance that cuts staff and has the true expectation that no ripples will be felt; that everyone can cinch up the belt and forge ahead without a change in work quality.

But it is a disastrous kind of arrogance when it is coupled with an already burned out staff, and a senior management team who doesn't believe in burnout.

BURN OUT

The term "burnout" is a relatively new term, first coined in 1974 by Herbert Freudenberger, in his book, *Burnout: The High Cost of High Achievement*. He originally defined 'burnout' as "the extinction of motivation or incentive, especially where one's devotion to a cause or relationship fails to produce the desired results."

Extinction. That is a very strong word. Freudenberger's definition says that burnout happens when the motivation to work towards a goal *ceases* to *exist*. Vanishes. Is eradicated.

Annihilated. Management theory has long stated that motivation is the key part of a strong performance by an employee; therefore, when an employee's motivation to perform their work is annihilated, doesn't that sound like something to which the leaders should pay attention?

Burned out employees feel ineffective, as though their contribution at the workplace doesn't matter. And with prolonged burnout, they can become very cynical about even showing up to work. "What am I doing here?" becomes the everyday question.

Burnout is a form of exhaustion, and exhausted people cannot and do not and will not produce good work. When the leadership ignores the causes of burnout, the toxin spreads, and the pond grows inhabitable.

Sometimes, an individual in a healthy environment can burn themselves out, without being poisoned by the toxin. A driven employee with improper boundaries may become the single, isolated burned out employee in an otherwise healthy environment. But it is when the environment itself is unhealthy that the toxin is present--when the causes of burnout are begun from above, and spread from above, and ignored from above.

Employees who bring up this topic are often soundly chastised and labeled as whiners, or unappreciative of their opportunity "to work for such a great company." Sometimes their comments are accepted, but later discarded. Sometimes they are outright rejected as untrue or exaggerated accounts.

Burnout primarily affects an employee's emotional connection to their work. It can be as basic as no longer being able to get motivated to go to work, or to do the work once there. It can manifest itself in disconnectedness from the team or from the projects. A burned out employee is far more likely to maximize taking personal days and sick days just to avoid the office. Once the bank of vacation, sick days, and personal days is exhausted, the employee may show up for work, but barely get through the day. This sort of inattention to the work at hand is a clear symptom of burnout. It also is not the employee's fault.

Burnout can creep up without warning, when the demands of the job consistently exceed the employee's ability or time to shoulder the load. Leslie Andrews was leaving the office later and later each evening. Even so, she seemed to continually be dashing out the door with her work undone, or stuffed into a briefcase to be brought home, *after* a full day at the office. The continual effort to "catch up" was having a detrimental effect on her ability to concentrate on the many projects at hand. It was also seriously cutting into her family life and creating tension at home. Her work was suffering, her marriage was strained, and she couldn't seem to shake a sense of tiredness. On Monday morning, when she pulled up her Outlook calendar, the culprit was clear: she actually had over 30 hours of meeting time allocated for the upcoming week. As she thought back over the previous month, she considered all the last minute meetings she'd been asked to be a part of, or had gotten dragged into. No wonder the work itself never got done!

The sense of disconnectedness created by the Toxin of Ignoring Burnout can spread from the work environment to personal pursuits. One executive trying to survive in a very toxic pond noticed that his emotional distancing had crept into his personal life and his hobbies. When he finally did have a little time off, he couldn't even muster the strength to enjoy his after-work hobbies. He had no enthusiasm for much of anything. This spread of burnout from the work environment to the rest of the employee's life is particularly poisonous. The Toxin had infected not just the work place, but him as well, and it traveled home with him when he shut the office door for the evening.

The spread of the toxin can poison the employee's home life and their health. Burned out employees experience an increase in illness and do not allow themselves time to recover from stressful experiences. This vicious cycle produces a downward spiral that results in poor productivity, poor morale, decreased effectiveness for the company, and ultimately, decreased profits.

The team becomes simply emotionally exhausted. As one employee said, "I just can't care about it anymore. I do whatever they tell me and go home at the end of the day. I mean, they don't really care about us anyway."

BURNED TO A CRISP

An emergency room surgeon who is on call nights and weekends has an expectation that he will be roused from sleep on occasion to perform his duties. Life-threatening accidents and illnesses cannot be scheduled, and therefore, neither can his hours at the office always be tidy and held between 8 and 5.

But very few business "emergencies" are true emergencies. We live in world where waiting for the microwave to heat up dinner for two minutes is painfully long. In the corporate environment, immediacy has somehow been tied to effectiveness. The faster we go, the faster we tackle the problem, and the faster the solution is brought forward somehow makes the accomplishment feel stronger.

As a result, communication no longer knows any boundaries. There was a time when the home was a place *away* from the office. Once the worker was in his home, he was *not at work*. With instant access has come the expectation of availability. Because we can email or send Blackberry messages 24/7, the expectation is that we'll be ready and watching, waiting for the communication to tell us what we must next do.

Even the family vacation has become compromised. What used to be a retreat from work, and a time of bonding for the family, has now become simply an office further away. "Are you taking your laptop on your trip?" is a common question the day the employee departs for vacation.

Requiring employees to be on call all of the time, regardless of personal or family commitments is simply a disastrous way to run a company. When the "always available" behavior is set from the top and reinforced from the top, the staff can feel powerless to fight it. Everyone becomes trained to be accessible at all times.

There's almost *always* another way for the problem to get solved. Amazingly enough, waiting until regular business hours generally works. All immediacy really does is satisfy the leader's ego that his people are at his beck and call, and will jump when he says so. He is functioning as a dictator with subjects who serve at his pleasure, rather than as a leader who brings a team together to accomplish a common goal.

This toxin can become so poisonous that even when employees are truly ill, they feel the need to come to work, compelled by a sense of fear that their job may be in jeopardy should they stay home. It is only the health of the colleagues who are now exposed to the sick worker that is truly in jeopardy. Being burned to a crisp is the feeling that the life has truly been sucked out of you by your job.

THE DEVALUATION OF TALENT

Leaders who do not value individual talents often overlook the particular and specific talents of their staff. Many executives want to believe everyone is interchangeable. Holding to this belief allows them to treat their staff any way they choose, including *mis*treating them, since in their minds all it takes to replace that individual is another warm body with a "better attitude." This mindset keeps the ends justified for the egotistic leader when the means by which he treats his staff are questionable.

Or, the leader may believe that if they only had enough time they could do that job too. This mindset is a common rationalization for not respecting an individual's *individual* contribution, and the specific talent they bring to the work.

It's also easy for a leader to unconsciously overload an employee with work, when the leader may not fully understand the requirements of executing that particular job. When the employee cannot perform the work in the timeframe or with the resources provided, she may work through to burnout in an effort to "get it done." But part of being a good leader is understanding the resources necessary for successful execution.

Everyone has to do some work that is tedious or boring to them no matter what the job description. But when an individual has to continually work in their areas of weakness or struggle, and never gets to shine in their core competencies, they will eventually burnout. Leaders who devalue the talent of their teams spread the Toxin of Ignoring Burnout.

LACK OF APPRECIATION

Individuals need to feel a sense of achievement. To do so, they must have discretion and power over their jobs. If the leaders view the employees as needing to be "corralled" or "watched" so they don't waste time, that attitude will never empower employees to solve their own problems or take ownership over their tasks. The Toxin of Ignoring Burnout not only devalues time and effort, it also fails to appreciate the work others are willing to give. When employees go the extra mile and perform good work., they must feel genuine acknowledgment from their bosses, or burnout starts to creep in.

The creative team for a promising start-up met at 4:30 pm Thursday to consider how it might be possible to revise the catalog according to the CEO's instructions and still meet the press deadline, which was Friday evening for a Saturday morning run. With the support of their Director, they decided it would simply take staying up all night to get it done. The Marketing Director knew the young team would need his direction throughout the process, so he brought in pizza and stayed with them. The team made the best of it, playing music as they worked. When dawn arrived, they actually all learned things about one another and had developed a better appreciation for each other. But the catalog wasn't finished yet.

The Marketing Director sent the team home in shifts during the next morning and afternoon, but stayed himself through the entire process to make sure it was finished on-time, and accurate. He also had to finalize the files and prepare them for delivery to the press. After a solid 36 hours without sleep, he finally left for home and the weekend to recuperate.

On Monday morning, the creative team gathered for coffee and comments. Though grumbling when it began, they now all felt great about their project accomplishment, and were proud to have kept the delivery date intact, even with the changes. They ribbed each other about the night with good-natured barbs.

The CEO walked into the room, the catalog proof in her hand, and the team turned to her. Who knows what they were expecting? If you had been on that team and done that work, what would you be expecting? The CEO, with disappointment clearly displayed in her face and in her voice, stated matter-of-factly, "If you'll do it my way next time, this won't happen again." She turned and walked out. The team was stunned, with one young designer actually taking a step backward in shock.

The fastest and best way to crush a team's sense of accomplishment is to criticize a major effort instead of praising it. Failure to appreciate the efforts of the team spreads the Toxin of Ignoring Burnout *beyond* out of control. Two simple words, *thank you*, can go a long way towards stemming the spread. But for some leaders, these are often the hardest two words in the English language to spit out. Some leaders don't praise their teams because they have the attitude of "Hey, that's what I pay you for." This leader is overlooking both basic human nature, and a very inexpensive way to keep employees happy.

Whether it is insecurity or ego that prevents a heartfelt *thank you* from being expressed, the withholding of appreciation is common from top leaders. One CEO remarked, "If I praise them for something they do right, then they won't feel the weight of the things they do wrong. So I just don't say anything." This CEO is poisoning the very company he started with this thinking.

Some leaders understand the *need* to appreciate the team's efforts, but can't genuinely convey it. But it is a fact of life that you cannot fake authenticity; empty praise is felt by the employees for what it is—false.

THE UNBALANCED WORKLOAD

Though chronic overwork can be a factor, burnout is generally the result of several stressors at the office, accompanied by a sense of resignation that things will never change. Loss of hope that things will be different is a clear indicator that the Toxin of Ignoring Burnout is spreading and infecting the pond inhabitants. Lack of hope is what sends talented employees to recruiters, looking for healthier ponds in which to work.

The truth is that a united and loyal team can tackle projects and events with gusto, as long as they know everyone will be treated with appreciation and a fair day off at the end. The occasional "All heave to" can even be looked forward to as a bonding event that provides employee stories for years. Properly managed, periods of excessive work can produce great memories. "Remember the time we had to stay up all night and re-design the catalog! What a night!" Poorly managed, the event becomes another sour experience, proving to the employees that their loss of hope in change is justified.

Employees need a balance of several factors to create a workplace in which they feel secure, and to which they can apply their best effort. Stability, fairness, respect, appreciation, recognition, *and* an appropriate workload are just some of the factors necessary for a healthy environment.

Powerlessness is a debilitating negative. When Kelly was expected to pick up the workload for her department when she was already chronically stressed, she felt powerless, both in controlling her health *and* accomplishing her job. In her situation, the managers were never told what criteria were used to manage the staff cuts; therefore, everyone assumed they could be next. Kelly had no assurance that she could influence her department, or even any security that she wouldn't be let go at any moment.

Unfortunately for the organization and the bottom line revenue, the most talented employees at the company are the ones who feel the burnout the most, because they are the most highly engaged workers. Highly connected to their work, talented employees simply aren't comfortable in an environment in which they cannot make a valuable contribution. They generally have options for good employment elsewhere, and eventually will seek them out. The most talented employees cost the most to replace, since they not only earn more, but have more experience, wisdom, and applicable knowledge.

Once an employee becomes burned out, it is easy for the leaders to marginalize her, believing her burnout to be for personal reasons. In order to prevent facing the reality of situation, the leaders must convince themselves her "failure" had nothing to do with the organization as a whole. Unfortunately for the company, this self-blinding leadership will continue to churn through talent like a revolving door.

It is part of the leader's job to watch out for the employees, to not overload them or exploit them. It was a Friday afternoon, and the Christmas party was about to begin for this 250 employee company. Karaoke, food, fun, gifts, and even silly games had made the annual event a favorite for the employees. But the CEO had ordered up new financials for the upcoming Monday board meeting from his Finance Director, Abi Dickson, and her team. It was a last minute decision he had come to in a brainstorm while driving to the office that morning.

Abi had participated in the karaoke contest the year before, and was really looking forward to the party. It was a hoot to see fellow workers in a more relaxed setting, and revealing parts of their personality rarely seen at work. But by the time the party had started, she and her team weren't nearly done with the CEO's new request. She had a choice between skipping the Christmas party, or canceling her weekend plans to get this work done. This was the first weekend she was going to have off in six weeks, so she definitely knew she wasn't going to come in. But she so hated missing the party, too! But Abi was a professional, and her work quality mattered to her. She knew the amount of time it would take to properly fill the CEO's request, and she would never turn in sloppy work. She skipped the Christmas party.

Sometimes an employee can be caught in such an unbalanced cycle, that they don't even realize it or know how to break it. Tony Stewart, constantly on the road training the company's sales force, received an email from Human Resources telling him he had reached the maximum accrual in vacation time and wouldn't receive any more until he took some of what he had. But Tony's managers could only see the work that had to be done, and never encouraged him to take time off, even though it was his to take. Because Tony traveled across the country for his job and didn't sit behind a desk, he felt obligated to stay on the move. *After all, does time spent in an airport really count as work?* he wondered. Well, it certainly doesn't count as vacation, does it? It's up to Tony's boss to help him manage his particular job circumstances, and find the appropriate balance. Ignoring the issue perpetuates the spread of the Toxin.

WHY IT MATTERS

Remember the old adage "Life is too short to...._____." Fill in the blank with what you don't want to miss. Life is certainly too short to live in a state of burnout when there are so many ways to make a living. Burnout steals zeal for life and saps away the pursuits that once interested you that aren't even work related.

Exhaustion is the state of something being used up completely. Burned out employees are exhausted—they have used up their passion, commitment, mental capacity, creative ability, and any other compelling or invigorating reason they come to work. How then will they be able to provide the best customer service, the best application of knowledge, the best construction of products, the best of anything? They can't, and ultimately, the business loses productivity, profitability, and a sustained future.

TO LEARN HOW TO REMOVE DEADLY TOXIN 3: IGNORING BURNOUT FROM YOUR WORKPLACE, READ CLEAN UP 2: CELEBRATE AND GIVE CREDIT.

Deadly Toxin 3 Poison Control:
Are you ignoring burnout?
Your particular circumstances may not resemble the ones discussed here, but surely there are ways to improve your pond. Answer these two questions to explore ways your pond may be toxic. If you are very brave, have your staff answer them as well!

1. Evaluate yourself and your staff for signs of burnout. Start with your staff job descriptions and measure them against your expectations. Does each of your staff members carry a reasonable load? How do you go about determining what is reasonable? List your criteria.

2. Do your employees have a balance between their work life and the rest of their life? Do they take their allowable vacation times and "unplug" from the office? If the answer is "no", what steps can you take to move your department in the right direction?

Deadly Toxin 4: Measuring by Method

Not everything that can be counted counts; and not everything that counts can be counted.

--Albert Einstein

Ann Duncan settled in her chair, laptop open, her slim fingers poised above the keyboard, ready to finish the one weekly task she most dreaded: the Friday report for the CEO.

Ann didn't dislike reports in general; in fact, the reports she generated or required from her staff provided valuable information that the team needed to keep the business moving forward. But *this* report.....

The intercom buzzed. "Mr. Adams wants to see you right away."

"Darn it," Ann thought to herself. "He got to me before I finished."

Mr. Adams is the CEO of a Midwest food manufacturing company. He hired Ann six years before, when the company was a start-up, and a multimillion-dollar annual revenue level was still a glimmer in his eye.

Ann is the Senior Vice President of Sales, managing all of the "front-facing" elements of the company such as the sales force, the media, and communications. She also has worked hand in hand with the Human Resources department to build a strong company for the employees. She has been instrumental in developing the internal culture of respect and integrity, as well as in orchestrating the efforts of the other departments to support the company's explosive growth.

Overall, Ann is very satisfied with her professional accomplishments at this company. And the top line dollars prove her work has been effective.

But this weekly report! Mr. Adams requires it from her as well as the rest of the Senior Team Executives. The report must recount every pertinent phone call, every email issue, and the details of each meeting they each conduct or attend. Due Fridays at noon. Ann often wonders what positive work goes undone because of the time they all spend compiling these tedious details. She's tried to tackle the issue before.

"Mr. Adams," she once said, "You can gain a very clear understanding of where the company stands each week by reviewing the success indicators report. It will tell you everything you need to know about each department."

"Ann," Mr. Adams smiled, and leaned back in his chair. "As I have said before, those reports are fine, but they don't provide me with the level of detail I *really* need to know to stay on top of the business."

"But Mr. Adams, they will tell you....." Ann halted in mid-sentence as Mr. Adams held up his hand in a stop-sign gesture.

"Frankly, Ann, I need to see those details from all of my Senior Executives, to make sure you are all focusing on the right things. The report lets me know that everyone is really doing what they are supposed to be doing-- that's all." The discussion was over.

Ann sighed and hit the intercom to tell her assistant, "I'm on my way." She printed the unfinished report and headed out the door, wondering how much longer she could bear working there.

TELLTALE TOXIC SIGNS

Ann has been so busy implementing processes and helping to manage the company's explosive growth that she hadn't noticed this report was merely a sign of something bigger--a toxin that had been growing in the pond since the company's beginning: The Toxin of Measuring by Method.

Mr. Adams had always been very involved in the details of the company, but it seemed to be worsening as the company grew larger. It was almost as if every new customer took him one step further away from his ability to maintain control over the organization he'd begun. He was increasingly nervous about exactly what his employees were doing--especially those who had the power and authority to make decisions.

He settled on a process that gave him the comfort level he wanted: the detailed weekly report. This report allowed him to "see" into all the phone conversations and emails that his staff had on the issues, so he could "stay in touch." Mr. Adams didn't know that he was responsible for spreading poison within his own pond.

At first, Ann and the rest of team thought it was a little strange that he'd rather see this sort of detail than judge their efforts by the Strategic Success Indicator numbers that they'd all worked to create, but they did it anyway--after all, he's the CEO, they'd said to each other.

But now, after grinding out those details week after week after week, they were all feeling weighed down by the report. Ann was beginning to understand that the report was simply one way Mr. Adams could micromanage the business through them, but avoid being labeled that way. After all, he'd say, it was *just* a report.

WHEN THE HOW MATTERS MORE THAN THE WHAT

When leaders have outlined a plan, but feel the need to also set the procedure for finding a solution, AND monitor the details of the execution, AND don't listen to the Team's input or use their expertise, then the Toxin of Measuring by Method is at work and spreading poison in the pond.

Micromanaging is the more common buzzword used today to describe this Toxin. This toxin is especially deadly to the most talented employees in the pond, because they have a very strong desire to contribute, which includes the ability to think through a problem and create a solution, without being told HOW to do so.

The Toxin of Measuring by Method is driven by fear-based insecurity, paranoia, and perfectionism. Seeking perfection is just another way of being dissatisfied with the efforts of others toward a goal. It's an excuse for the leader to become overly involved.

Measuring by Method is repressive management, meaning that it keeps a lid on any talent. The most talented employees are the ones who have the highest need to contribute at their workplace, which includes the freedom to tackle and solve problems. The micromanaging leader's need to control the how of what gets done frustrates the efforts of those working on the problem because it prevents them from fully engaging, and it destroys the self-esteem of the employee trying to satisfy them. When nothing they produce is satisfactory or ever accepted as good enough, it takes a toll.

ORGANIZATIONAL STRUCTURE

A century ago, organizational structure did not exist for anyone outside the family, the military or the church. Professionals and trade smiths generally worked alone, or with an apprentice or clerk.

It was German economist and sociologist Max Weber, after observing the organizational innovations of the German leader Bismark in the late 1800's, who first identified a new kind of organization for large groups of people.

Weber thought he could structure the "ideal" organization built along lines of structure, formality, and hierarchy. He wanted to produce a structure that would continue to function whether or not the personnel changed, and built the structure on functionality, rather than on personality.

His ideas are the basis for the formal organization chart that most everyone has seen and operated under at some point. Traditionally, the organization was headed by a Chief Executive Officer, and the other divisions and departments were bundled up under the Chief Operating Officer (COO) and the Chief Financial Officer (CFO). As organizations grew more complicated in their sales and marketing efforts, new "C-Level" positions have been added. It's not uncommon to see a Chief Marketing Officer (CMO) for example.

For the past several decades, many sorts of organizational designs have been put in place to try to minimize the formality and rules of the traditional system to allow for more movement and open communication between departments and divisions. Additional "C's" have been invented—Chief People Officer or Chief Creative Officer, for example.

Some organizations, understanding the need for some sort of structure, but wanting to get far away from the formality of the hierarchy, give their roles names such as Big Kahuna or Top Dog instead of CEO, or Director of First Impressions for the receptionist.

The point is that every organization needs a structure in which to operate. Organizational structure is simply a mechanism to divide up the tasks of the business, in order to produce measurable results and meet the company's objectives. The structure is put in place to ensure that work is not duplicated, and that objectives are met with the smallest amount of friction or misunderstanding.

Structure provides a guideline, and a protection—it's a boundary, a fence line that reminds the organization that processes are in place for getting work done. Appropriate boundaries in the workplace are a *good* thing.

Another key component to employee satisfaction is education and opportunity to learn and grow, and advance in the company. But by implication, a leader who manages by method does not see the value in education, because education is meant to empower and equip the employee in MORE concentrated efforts for problem solving and moving the business forward with creative thought and work. Because the leader doesn't value it, it likely won't be promoted at work, or there will be promises of it coming, but it will never materialize.

Giving it lip service is worse than ignoring it all together. Lip service destroys hope, and hope is what fuels the human tank—without hope, everything else dwindles away. But it is a rare leader who can recognize their own shortcomings and see clearly enough in the mirror to make self-corrections.

When the drive for personal power and personal achievement outweigh the drive to influence employees to meet the organization's needs and objectives, then Measuring by Method becomes a standard practice. When it becomes a standard practice, the poison grows and the pond inhabitants get sicker and sicker.

FAILURE TO DELEGATE

The clearest sign that the Toxin of Measuring by Method is present in the pond centers around delegation. To delegate means handing over *responsibility* for an outcome with the requisite *authority* and *decision-making power* necessary to get the job done. Whatever the structure of the business, employees are hired to move the business forward. In order to do so, the leaders must delegate work to them.

Failure to delegate creates a culture of fear and insecurity among the employees. Nobody is willing to cross the line, to take a stand, make a contribution, or solve a problem.

They know they will get their hand slapped or worse, endure public criticism, so instead they pile up outside the boss' door waiting for the answer because that's the environment the leader has set up, often while complaining that they can't get anything done, or that no one will make a decision.

It's not uncommon to hear the micromanaging leader say, "I wouldn't have to be so involved if I had the right people." If the leader is building or rebuilding a structure, this may be valid. But if it becomes the excuse for never letting go of work and empowering the team to function with autonomy, it simply is an admission of micromanaging. In the same way, if a leader is constantly harassed by unexpected emergencies, it's because that leader hasn't given direct reports the ability to solve problems on their own and come to the table with solutions, regardless of the method. When emergencies become commonplace, they no longer bear the definition of an emergency. Instead, it's just poor management.

Micromanaging leaders tend to believe they cannot ever find employees fit for the job, and that really if they only had the time they'd do it better themselves. This is rarely the real truth. Talent abounds in all organizations. The failure is in the leadership to recognize it, leverage it, promote it, not be intimidated by it, and put it to work. Failure to do so only serves the dictatorial nature of the leader, not the organization.

"If you want something done right, do it yourself" should *never* be the mantra of a leader in an organization. Retaining control of details spreads the Toxin of Measuring by Method, and it is destructive to creative problem solving.

The act of delegation doesn't end with handing over the project to a qualified employee. The appropriate follow through for delegation is to allow the *outcome* to determine whether the execution was poor or good. Anything less is subversive because it creates the appearance that employees will have ownership over the job and the process, but keeps all really important tasks and decisions with the leader who doesn't want to let go. In the end, the micromanager's decision may simply be a matter of preference.

Tim entered his office after the meeting, shutting the door behind him. He stood there for a minute, still holding the door handle and said out loud to no one, "Why did she even ask me to work on this project? I could have spent all those hours working on something else instead of spending time researching a topic she already had decided on!"

Tim had just submitted information he had gathered about meeting sites for an upcoming event. He was excited to be a part of the planning team and it was a new opportunity for him as an Events Manager. His boss had given him the budget, explained the purpose of the event, and what she was looking for in a location. Tim hit the ground running and began his research.

But Tim's boss didn't really trust Tim to pick the right location. *After all,* she reasoned, *Tim is new to this and may make a mistake that would embarrass me. It's critical that the important decisions around this project remain under my control to ensure the best outcome.*

So Tim's boss decided that she would look at a few places also, you know, just in case. She found the perfect spot, and had it ready as a "back up" if Tim failed to come through.

When Tim gave his presentation, he had found several locations that matched the specifications the boss had outlined. But in the end, the boss was more satisfied with her own choice than with Tim's work. She told Tim, "I appreciate the work you put into your presentation, but I am really happy with this location." Tim felt sabotaged, and indeed he was. Tim's choices fit all of the criteria; any one of his choices would have sufficed. But the boss couldn't let go.

KILLING THE DRIVE OF THE MOST TALENTED EMPLOYEES

There is no better way to kill the drive of talented employees than to take away their opportunity to become deeply involved in creative problem solving. For the talented employee, the joy and satisfaction comes from having ownership over the project, and from investing themselves emotionally in the process.

Using their creativity and particular talent, they find the satisfaction in the effort as much as in the outcome. When a leader critiques the work on HOW it was done, rather than on what results were achieved, the leader is attacking the best part of the employee's work.

When subordinates know that their ideas or solutions won't be accepted, they stop bringing them to the table. For the boss, this may feel like the employees have no initiative, but truly it's because they know they won't be recognized as valid. There will always be a reason why it's not good enough, or needs work, or needs to go back to the drawing board. It's a situation the leader creates and sustains.

All objectives are met by the accomplishment of smaller tasks along the way. The tasks can very often be put on a timeline and checklist, and as each one is checked off, the project moves closer to completion. But there is so much more to the work than a checklist! Pride of ownership, personal satisfaction and personal achievement are the intangibles that employees are truly seeking through their work. These things are not built by checking off *someone else's* checklist. Talented employees must have the freedom to make their own list as part of the creative problem solving process. Creating their own list to determine the HOW is part of what empowers them and provides satisfaction.

LACK OF TRUST MANAGEMENT

The CEO of a large insurance company knew he had to do something about the sagging morale in the office. He decided to set up an Advisory Committee made up of employees from different departments and at different levels of rank to consider issues, employee complaints, and to plan some fun activities throughout the year.

The nominated employees were thrilled to get to be on the committee and were totally committed and excited about the opportunity to contribute to their workplace and make it great. But about six months after it was formed, the group had pretty much disbanded, and the CEO was highly disappointed. He couldn't quite put his finger on why this had happened. Some of the committee resigned their positions, others just stopped showing up for the meetings. "Well," he reasoned, "it just goes to show that the employees themselves don't really know what's best for the company."

Far from it.

The Advisory Committee had simply believed that they had been empowered to accomplish what they had been told was their responsibility—but each suggestion they made was rejected by the Senior Team for one reason or another, and each problem they addressed could not be solved for one reason or another. The entire committee began to understand that they were merely an ornament, window dressing, and that they actually had no substantive authority to implement anything at all. One by one they drifted away.

As the Toxin spreads, employees are less and less willing to offer solutions, feeling "what's the point?" Either the boss will do it his way anyway, or there will be another reason why nothing can change. When the leaders don't listen, or even worse, appear to listen but never implement anyone's suggestions but their own, the distrust spreads.

The leaders in the business sometimes run their organizations from fear, and frankly, there is much to fear about the running of a business. Fear that the work won't get done well or right. Fear that poorly done work will reflect on them unfavourably. Fear that the organization will fail and that they may be blamed. Fear of this, that, and the other. There are multiple opportunities for fear to take hold, and leaders are susceptible to all of them.

This fear often drives leaders to assume the worst with their employees. Their expectation is that the employees come to work grudgingly. Or that they come to take advantage, or show up for a pay check only, or in some other way are just waiting around to cause some harm to the business. Though truly unwarranted, this fear fuels the spread of the Toxin of Measuring by Method. What the leaders fail to recognize is that they are creating a climate ripe for failure by allowing fear to dictate their management methods.

People come to work intent on doing a good job. Leaders destroy talent all the way down the chain of command to the lowest staff level person when they assume they don't. The leaders' fear creates an environment of mistrust. Employees stop sharing valuable information with each other, stop communicating, and generally become more apathetic about their jobs. As in the case above with the Advisory Committee, the failure is a self-fulfilling prophecy for the CEO.

PURSUING THE COLLECTIVE GOOD

The Toxin of Measuring by Method is much more concerned about controlling the employee's behavior than it is about producing good work that moves the business forward.

During the Enlightenment (1762), Rousseau observed that institutions could only flourish if they are founded on a social contract that enables human beings to pursue their individual and collective interests to the fullest extent possible. This French philosopher knew then what we emphasize in successful organizations today: The modern enterprise flourishes when there is attention to and respect for the human beings who contribute their work efforts.

There is no simple formula. There is no answer in a box or software program that can solve this problem. Only the careful application of sound judgment, working on a bedrock foundation of respect for people can wipe out this poison.

Managing the humanity of people is the critical part of good leadership. Doing a good job of this can give any company a keen competitive advantage, as the creativity of its people are actively engaged in problem solving. But the Toxin of Measuring by Method prevents this advantage as the advances of the company become limited by the methods of accomplishment acceptable to the leader. This Toxin often doesn't accept the very thing that could move a business ahead in their industry: creative problem solving. Creative problem solvers have to be free to work without limits, focusing only on the outcome as they devise the solution.

WHY IT MATTERS

When the leader believes that his way is the only right way, and hires individuals who support and endorse his self-image, he is spreading the Toxin of Measuring by Method, and making sure that his Senior Team does as well.

Senior level employees should not be involved in hubcap selection for fleet trucks, reviews of managerial expense accounts, or sales meetings recaps. Nor should they be involved in copy editing, in word choice, or photo selection. If your employees cannot do this work for you, find new employees. If you cannot find new employees, then you need to realize the common denominator in all your poor employee performance is you.

TO LEARN HOW TO REMOVE DEADLY TOXIN 4: MEASURING BY METHOD FROM YOUR WORKPLACE, READ CLEAN UP 3: BUILD COMMUNITY.

Deadly Toxin 4 Poison Control:
Are you measuring by method?
Your particular circumstances may not resemble the ones discussed here, but surely there are ways to improve your pond. Answer these two questions to explore ways your pond may be toxic. If you are very brave, have your staff answer them as well!

1. When my employees finish a project that meets expectations in results, but isn't the way I would have done it, I _____ (fill in the blank).

2. What measures can I take in my area at work to ensure that my employees are able to contribute to the best of their ability?

Deadly Toxin 5: Constant Fast

It is not enough to be busy; so are the ants.
The question is: what are we busy about?

--Henry David Thoreau

Susan Cummings, an accomplished copywriter in the creative department of a large, mid-western textiles company, leaned back in her chair absentmindedly tapping her armrest, taking a minute to yawn and stretch. Susan had been arriving an hour early every day for the past two weeks, working through lunch most days, and generally leaving about 30 minutes late as well. Before these two weeks, she'd been giving up weekends for months, and was hoping this schedule would give her back Saturday and Sunday. She and her husband had been fighting lately about all the time she was putting in, and she had spent a small fortune on extra babysitting for their 3-year old while her husband was at work on Saturdays. Besides, she was missing too much of her daughter's life! Something had to give.

She had asked her boss when they'd be hiring another writer, as the workload was too much for one person to perform the best quality work. And producing good work was important to Susan. She prided herself on the awards she'd won for her writing, and for the care she put into the writing projects assigned to her. Her boss let her know there were no plans to add another writer to the department through the end of the year. "It's not in the budget," he'd said. "It's up to you to get it done."

She stretched her arms over her head and sighed. Jared, a graphics designer and cube neighbor, heard the sigh and popped his head over the top of the wall, taking a break from his own job to share her frustration. She said to him, "I'm so tired from working at this pace for so many months, I'm too exhausted to care about the work anymore."

"What about all those promises that things were going to slow down?" asked Jared. "I know I've heard it from the boss at least three times."

"Oh, I've stopped paying attention to what they say," sighed Susan. "It's like the story of the boy who cried 'wolf'— you just stop hearing it because you know it won't be true," she said, sitting up straight and taking a deep breath. "Well, I have to finish this if I want to avoid coming in on Saturday. Back to work."

"At least you have the option," mumbled Jared as he turned back to his desk. "I'll be here both Saturday and Sunday to finalize the design on these materials for the new promotions."

Jared's words struck Susan hard. She realized that over time everyone's workload had increased to beyond reasonable--not just hers. She realized if anything were going to change, it would be up to her. She could remember when these crazy hours started—eight months ago on the promotional campaign for the new product launch. The creative team had come together and produced a stellar campaign for that product, rocketing it to fabulous sales. But there was a toll on the team—they'd put in nights and weekends for over three months to get it developed to perfection. It's as if once management got a taste of that accelerated speed of work, they'd decided the normal pace was just too slow. They now needed the team to function at this "peak" performance all the time, so that they could move up the production cycle and get a lot more done in less time.

Nobody on the creative team saw that coming! How could they know that their burst of creative energy and passion, targeted to one specific campaign, would become the new standard for normal? How could they know their reward for excellent results would be more work?

Susan decided that as soon as their daughter was asleep tonight, she'd start looking online for another job. She didn't want to leave her position—she loved her job—but her family came first, and if management thought this pace of work was something she could keep up all the time instead of reserving as a "call to action" for occasional projects, they had another think coming.

Suddenly, she felt a little less burdened, just giving herself the hope that soon she might be out of this crazy pace.

TELLTALE TOXIC SIGNS

Susan was growing sick from the spread of a poison at her workplace. The Deadly Toxin of Constant Fast was taking hold. She came to understand her situation would not change. The expectation from the leadership was that she and her co-workers would do whatever was necessary to develop and implement the projects the executives sent down the pipe.

Susan was not the only employee feeling pressure from home with the increased hours and expectations. Other spouses and families had been accepting at first, as the promise was that the extra hours were just temporary. But The Toxin of Constant Fast had indeed taken hold, spreading throughout the pond and poisoning the organization, while the tension generated in the families of the employees was also growing.

In Susan and Jared's situation, the leadership had become addicted to a rapid pace during the execution of a great campaign. "If this is the kind of work the team produces with a fire under them," reasoned the CEO, "Let's keep the fire burning all the time!"

Other companies may find themselves spreading the Toxin of Constant Fast in their ponds by trying to compete, keep up, adjust to sales dips, and plain forge ahead. The Toxin can begin with the organization, or creep upon it in stages. To complicate matters, once the Toxin of Constant Fast spreads through the organization, it can occasionally produce good results. Going back to a slower pace can feel like wasting time by contrast. It can become addicting for some managers and CEO's who lose sight of the fact that humans simply aren't wired for Constant Fast.

FAST, CHEAP, OR GOOD, BUT NOT ALL THREE

Every organization wants to produce quality work quickly, and at a good price. But these are all relative terms. How good is quality? How fast is quickly? What's a good price? Of course, it depends upon the nature of the project, and the resources available. An IT development project will necessarily take more time than designing a new brochure. Outsourcing creative talent can cost more than in-house talent. Quality may be the most arbitrary of all—one man's treasure is another man's garbage and so forth. With all of these variables, how do you make sure you receive quality work, quickly, and at a good price?

In truth, satisfying all three may be impossible. It is a standard rule in business that in any given work scenario, you can only achieve two out of these three: Fast, Cheap, Good. If the timeline is Fast, and the budget is Cheap, you won't get Good. If you want Fast and Good, you definitely won't get Cheap. Fast and Good is expensive. And Good doesn't ever really come Cheap. At the rapid and ridiculous pace of Constant Fast, you lose all three.

THE NEED FOR CHAOS

The Toxin of Constant Fast is often spread through organizations by executives and high-level managers who have a need to create chaos. There are simply some individuals who function better when the stakes are high and everyone is in a titter deciding and executing last minute changes.

Often those creating the chaos have no idea the toll it takes on the team executing the dictates. The executive decides a change is warranted and then moves on to other issues, while the team scrambles to execute the details. Or the executive simply doesn't care that a massive effort is necessary, as he feels the change in decision or direction is worth whatever effort it takes to make it happen. "Make it happen," is the mantra of the chaotic leader.

"Boss, we have very limited resources to execute that request," may be the plea of a manager who can see the Toxin's work of ruin ahead. "Make it happen!" is the commanding reply.

"Ah, the last envelope!!" exclaimed Connie Heron, nearly giddy from exhaustion and the awareness that this was the absolute last time today she'd have to stuff these envelopes with flyers and brochures. They'd begun the project at 8:30 am this morning, and were finally finishing up close to 6:00 pm. It had been a long day of collating and stuffing for Connie and the other six employees around the table, piled high with stacks from which they drew the appropriate number of papers and sorted them into three different envelopes.

Twice a year, Connie's company held a big sales meeting geared to motivate their national sales force. Employees signed up to work at the event. Though hard work, it was also fun and rewarding to see the sales force respond positively to the new initiatives launched for the year. The employees loved getting a first hand glimpse of the sales force, and to be reminded whom they are supporting by their own work back at the office.

This conference had been more stressful than previous ones Connie had volunteered for, however. The CEO had put several major initiatives in place in the six months prior to the conference, and the staff working the long hours at the event was the same staff that had been working long hours at the office for the past few months. They arrived fatigued.

Connie held her hands out in front of her, surveying her paper cuts. "Not too bad, I guess," she commented to Paul, standing next to her. "I don't have a band-aid on every finger!" But the shift was ending and now she could get some dinner. Her feet were killing her, and she was bleary-eyed from the day. That's when she and Paul heard Sheila, the Team Captain, shouting into her cell phone. "I will NOT tell these people to do that! They have been stuffing envelopes for nine hours in this room today...." the Team Captain practically threw the phone onto the table and stormed out of the room.

"What's going on?" the employees whispered to each other.

Sheila finally calmed down and returned to the small room where the Team was sitting—a little afraid to break for dinner till they knew what was happening.

"An executive decision has been made," said the Team Captain, rocking back and forth on her heels with her arms crossed above her chest, "to pull two handouts from the morning envelope and re-stuff them into a separate envelope. Since the morning session starts at 8:30 tomorrow, we'll have to do it tonight."

It's not that the process itself was difficult—and having just spent nine hours doing it, they were well trained. But this would not be a quick fix. The team had stuffed over 5,000 envelopes, and it had taken all day long. They were now being told basically to start over.

It's not that the team didn't want to work hard—after all, they were all volunteering to work hard just by being there! No, it was the feeling of wasted time and energy, of uselessness. As the shift had ended, everyone had felt good about the job they'd done, preparing for the next day's sessions and doing their part to equip the sales force.

Now because the same executive who'd already signed off a week ago on the project they'd executed this morning decided to make a last-minute change, the victory completely dissipated and was replaced with sagging exhaustion. "They couldn't have told us that this morning before we did all this work?" became the mumbled complaint.

Connie, Paul, and many others would debate before volunteering again for this event. It's not hard work they minded; it's being taken advantage of for someone else's need to be chaotic that they seriously minded.

THINKING COUNTS

Leaders who thrive on chaos cannot stand calm in their immediate team. A calm and ordered team means to them that something is going undone, because it is a state of being they do not share. In their minds, to be effective, they must be busy. They cannot understand that being busy does not necessarily equate to being effective.

In fact, in order to be most effective, the leaders of the organization must take time to think and reflect, to process and prioritize the business at hand. Failure to spend adequate time simply thinking about the business can spell disaster. But taking the time to think feels like wasted time to those infected with the Toxin of Constant Fast.

The COO of one company had implemented processes and procedures to run the business efficiently, and that gave him time in his day for research—reading, thinking, and keeping up with current operational trends. He would often spend one hour a day in this pursuit, sitting at his desk. His only mistake was in leaving his door open.

The CEO couldn't stand it! He commented to another executive, "I don't pay him to think. I pay him to run operations." For this executive, the lack of busyness and the presence of calm created strong objections. It felt like wasted time. Since he was sitting still reading, it couldn't possibly count as work.

But thinking IS the work! The work of clarifying roles, assigning objectives, working through a plan becomes the slow way to do things, and normal begins to look like inefficiency.

WHICH DIRECTION, WHERE?

When the Toxin of Constant Fast is spreading its poison, company direction often spins around like a broken weather vane. One minute north, another south, another minute west. Direction becomes a guess rather than a reality.

When the Senior Leaders aren't clear on company direction, how can anyone else be? Without clear direction, decision-making becomes a muddled mess from the executive level down to the lowest staff member.

But the business must move forward, so managers and staff make the best decisions they can as they try to fulfill their roles. Fear rules as no one is really willing to make a mistake or sign off on anything that might leave them holding the bag if the direction proves to be wrong. Decisions bottleneck as they wait to be made by one or two people in the building. Meanwhile, deadlines pass, and Constant Fast has once again sacrificed quality work, normal timelines, and the budget gets blown again.

In the pond where Constant Fast is spreading its poison, it's not uncommon for leaders to change the directive on a plan twice in the same afternoon. This sort of Constant Fast sets in motion a complex series of tactical actions, and if the project is large and involves more than one staff member or more than one department, the margin for error in keeping up with the changes goes through the roof.

In Constant Fast, what was important yesterday is superceded by what is important today. And sometimes, what was important this morning is superceded by what's important this afternoon.

Typically the only personality who has the luxury to perpetuate Constant Fast is a key decision maker, simply because they would never tolerate this behavior from someone who works for them. The Toxin of Constant Fast wreaks budgetary and operational havoc.

VENDOR RELATIONSHIPS SUFFER

The Toxin of Constant Fast also helps destroy the company's credibility. Producing programs or printed materials at the speed of Constant Fast increases errors in the materials. From a basic typo to a major guffaw, if after every program or announcement you have to send follow up materials correcting errors, you are spending more money, and teaching your customers to expect mediocrity.

And the vendor who must support the Constant Fast pace, and the correction process, including print, video producers, external creative, IT contractors, hotel managers, others, will grow increasingly uncomfortable working with your organization. The timeframes and revisions, changes, press times, commitments to their other clients will get you labeled a problem client, no matter how much money you may be willing to throw at the problem.

Print Coordinator Leslie Wynn's hand was literally shaking as she picked up the phone to call her printer, Bud Thomas. This was the third time she's had to call this week, struggling to nail down a press time for a catalog that the CEO kept changing. Leslie knew how frustrated her vendor was becoming. He had always been very loyal to Leslie's company, largely because he could count on Leslie's consistency in delivering on-time files.

But lately, Leslie was falling into the habits of some of his worst customers—scheduling a print date, then calling back to reschedule, then calling back to reschedule again! Bud was fortunate to have a solid print business, but that meant his presses were running constantly and maintaining the schedule was important to keep the machines from becoming idle. And idle press could cost him thousands of dollars a day—and rescheduling already scheduled press runs often resulted in idle presses as clients were bumped and pulled to make the accommodations.

"Bud, hi this is Leslie again….."

MIXED MESSAGES

The Toxin of Constant Fast breeds another phenomenon—the poison of mixed messages. Because sometimes what is said out loud and what everyone knows to be true are two different things. Marcy Thomas believes that her job is destroying her family life. She's working 60-hour weeks with no bonus or extra pay. Even on her days off, she is bombarded by emails and calls from work. The management does say, "Take off compensatory time," but regards the employees as uncommitted when they do. She's tried to talk to her bosses about the problem but nothing happens. The last straw came when the HR department launched a campaign encouraging healthy habits at work and home, and offering a discount at a local fitness center. "Leaving late every day leaves me no time to take advantage of it!" she fumed.

Marcy has reached the point that she's just started leaving at 6 p.m., no matter what, and has stopped checking voice- or email when she's home. But now she's worried that she is committing career suicide.

RESILIENCE AND MARGIN

Resilience is the ability to spring back into shape after being compressed, stretched or bent out of proper shape. Resilience is a necessary component of any healthy person or environment. Life is full of unexpected bumps and drops, times when accelerated effort is necessary. This is commonly called the "Fight or Flight" syndrome—those times when the amazing human system adapts to the extraordinary needs of the situation.

Resilience is a person's ability to recover from the Flight or Fight syndrome and become their natural state of productive again, at a normal pace. To continue to be productive over the long haul, each person must regain the strength and rebuild the reserves that will be necessary for the next Flight or Fight situation.

No one, animal or human, is programmed to remain in the state of "Flight or Fight" long-term. Existing there permanently does not allow any margin for rebuilding strength and recouping resistance.

Many jobs require crunch times--tax preparation in the spring, seasonal businesses at holiday times, any time during sales conventions or annual events. When the extra mile is required but monitored appropriately, it can be an extremely rewarding time—a team of people throws in, makes special arrangements, and devotes themselves to the accomplishment of the project—and great bonds are formed and the working relationships are strengthened. But it can't go on forever.

The Toxin of Constant Fast forces a Flight or Fight state of constancy. Continuing amounts of stress that should be "punctuations" of work become the norm. Constant fast doesn't allow recovery time before moving into the next project that also requires Constant Fast. And it's not just the load that contributes to the stress. Constant Fast produces errors, additional work, irritable attitudes, fights at home over long hours, and even missed "life-time" events such as children's activities and other personal commitments. The culmination of stressors doesn't slow down; therefore, the individual never slows down.

Instant communication makes people feel as if they should be continuing to communicate, during "after hours" weekends, and even on vacation. The standard "out of office reply" for many employees goes like this, "I am on vacation and won't be back until Monday. I have limited access to email, but will check when I can. My cell phone won't work in the remote area we are traveling to, so please call my assistant who can get in touch with me if it's an emergency."

These are only the kinds of messages you should leave with people in charge of your children. Your out of office message should read, "Gone. Be back Monday. Call Barry."

If the leaders or CEO are workaholics themselves, and simply expect the same from the employees, it's even tougher to battle this Toxin. "I never ask my employees to do anything I wouldn't do," is not a comfort if the leader is a 70-hour a week workaholic!

Leaders often make it to the front of the pack because of their ability to work faster, longer, and harder than anyone around them. This may get them recognized and promoted, but personal production rates are certainly not the only thing to consider when putting someone in charge of a team; in fact, it may the last thing to consider, given the objective of a leader is not at all the objective of a personal achiever.

STRESS KILLS ME

Cortisol and adrenaline are hormones produced by the adrenal glands that equip the body to either stand and fight the enemy, or turn in flight and get away safely. Amazing changes to the body occur spontaneously. The heart beats faster, pumping blood to the major muscle groups, digestion slows, and reaction times grow quicker, all in an effort to face the threat. Once the danger is gone, the body returns to normal function by relaxing, which causes the hormone levels recede.

The same hormones are activated in situations that don't require running away or standing and fighting—stress produces cortisol and adrenaline as well. That is why cortisol is sometimes called "the stress hormone."

When the perceived threat is gone, systems are designed to return to normal function via the relaxation response. But when the Toxin of Constant Fast is spreading in the pond, the un-ending pace doesn't allow the body to relax and return to the normal state. The hormones continue to dump into the body, but with no burst of energy to allow them to dissipate and do their work. Instead, they build up in our bodies, and can cause long-term physical damage.

The body can work off these extra hormones and return to a normal state by imposing exercise or meditative relaxation through hitting the gym, running, or taking a yoga class. But here again, the Toxin of Constant Fast spreads its poison as it leaves no time for these events to be scheduled. Every health practitioner advocates 30 minutes of exercise three to four times per week, as well as seven hours of sleep a night. But when dinner is rushed so that mom or dad can continue to work on a project, or taken up again after kids homework and bedtime, employees poisoned with the Toxin of Constant Fast cannot even retreat into their own homes and find time to relax.

WHY IT MATTERS

What separates us from the animals if not our imaginations, our joy, our abilities to love and plan our lives? For that matter, what separates us from the machines if we don't allow time in our lives for what matters? The Toxin of Constant Fast demands a brutal pace and humanity simply was not meant to function that way. Over time, employees will find a way to resume balance in their lives. Either their own poor health will force a choice, or they will leave for other jobs. Those who cannot leave will likely disengage and pull back in their enthusiasm, leaving a decimated work force that cannot produce the best quality work.

TO LEARN HOW TO REMOVE DEADLY TOXIN 5: CONSTANT FAST FROM YOUR WORKPLACE, READ CLEAN UP 4: EXERCISE CREATIVE DISCIPLINE.

Deadly Toxin 5 Poison Control:
Are you working at constant fast?
Your particular circumstances may not resemble the ones discussed here, but surely there are ways to improve your pond. Answer these two questions to explore ways your pond may be toxic. If you are very brave, have your staff answer them as well!

1. My staff works past closing time or on weekends ____ times per month. Over the past twelve months, this has equated to _____ times. My staff is comprised of ____ people. The total number of hours worked past normal hours in the last twelve months is

____.

2. I have changed deadlines ____ times in the last six months. Each change has required ____ more hours of work from the staff of ____ people (include staff in departments affected by the change who may not report to you—for example, support services departments.) The total number of additional hours over the last six months is _____.

Deadly Toxin 6: Revisiting Decisions

There is nothing so useless as doing efficiently that which should not be done at all.

--Peter Drucker

"Hi, thanks for coming down," said Alan Hanks, Vice President of Marketing for a large clothing catalog company. Alan's impressive background included work at Neiman's, and part of his job responsibility at this company was to manage the promotion of new products through the photography displayed in the catalog. He merchandised "the book" with the utmost care towards sales, tracking sales per page, analyzing the placement of items against their sales in increases or decreases, and confirming the positioning of key merchandise on the best "real estate" pages in the catalog. He prided himself on working closely with the merchants to ensure he was indeed promoting the appropriate products in this monthly catalog.

Alan was holding the catalog "war room" door open for his boss, Senior Vice President of Sales and Marketing, Allison Tish. They both walked into the room, where the pages of the newly-revised catalog were attached with sharp t-pins to fabric-covered walls.

He began, "We've made all of the changes you requested last week, even replacing the image on the front cover. I was afraid it might forfeit our press run time, but it looks as if our vendor can shift another client, and we'll just squeak in under the wire."

Alan was growing more and more concerned as the Senior Vice President seemed to be focusing once again on the front cover. This meeting was supposed to be a very brief final sign off, not one for changes! The team had been working in high gear for several days to shoot the new photography, and it truly was too late to make any additional changes *and* meet the press deadline.

"See?" he said. "We re-photographed it just as you said, with the model now to the left of the fireplace, and the curtains drawn a bit to cut down the lighting contrast."

Allison stood transfixed, clasping her hands together behind her back before the catalog pages on the wall. She said, "I'm just wondering if we made the right choice with that particular blouse….," her voice trailed off as she stared intently at the cover.

Alan was becoming desperate. His team was already discouraged by the mad scramble that was required whenever the Senior Vice President decided to get involved in the catalog photography. *Whose job was it, anyway?* they'd ask, offended that their boss wasn't trusted with making the decisions his job description required of him, and that his experience said he was good at.

Alan, trying to control the frustration in his voice, said out loud, "We'll never make the press deadline if you change it again."

"All right, I guess it's okay," she finally said as she signed her initials on the cover page. Alan knew without a doubt that the only thing preventing her from making additional changes was the truth of the deadline. She was simply unwilling to be responsible for the catalog being late.

Allison left the war room, and Alan stood silently for several minutes surveying the catalog pages pinned to the walls. He used to feel great on catalog sign-off day. He was proud of his team of photographers, stylists, copywriters and graphic artists. They would gather together in the war room and have a little celebration that included clapping and pats on the back for all involved.

For the last six months, that exultation had been replaced by dread, and the celebrations had quietly dwindled and died out as everyone realized over time that the Senior Vice President's last minute changes were her way of operating, not a one-time thing. She couldn't trust the team with the outcome of the catalog without getting involved in the smallest details, and she could never stick with the original plan, even when it was formulated by good data and sound judgment, even when she was the chief formulator! Today he wondered how long it would take him to update his resume.

TELLTALE TOXIC SIGNS

The proverb "actions speak louder than words" is burned into our collective psyches. And for a reason—because it's true! In this case, Alan's job description, defined by words on a page, said he was responsible for determining product placement within the catalog. But the repeated actions of the Senior Vice President voided those words every month as she inserted herself into the process. What was decided and signed off on in the beginning just became something else to change the closer the deadlines loomed.

What Alan didn't know was that he was living in a toxic environment, and he and his team were becoming sicker and sicker with the Toxin of Revisiting Decisions. What had been a cause for celebration was now a cause for dread, and the sparks of creativity were being drowned.

Alan was rightly concerned that his team was becoming de-motivated, as was he. Their collective discouragement couldn't help but manifest itself by less passion, less commitment, more daydreaming, more grumbling. Toxins make the inhabitants sick, and create an environment in which productive work becomes increasingly impossible. It is their nature.

In another pond in another city, the Toxin of Revisiting Decisions is also at work. Sarah Daniels, a talented web designer in the middle of a re-design for her company's web site, threw her head back against her chair in utter discouragement. "What is going on up there, anyway?" gesturing upstairs where the executives resided and where the decision had just been made to completely scrap the new website design the IT team had been working on for three months in favor of a completely different direction. "Can't anybody up there make up their minds?"

Tom, her cube mate, and co-designer on the now-dead web project, added, "What I'm doing isn't making a difference anyway. As soon as I finish something, they throw it all away. Why should I continue to try my hardest? It's just too discouraging."

When the employees feel that their efforts don't matter towards the overall accomplishment of the company's goals, the toxin of Revisiting Decisions is effectively working.

RESPONSIBILITY AND AUTHORITY

Responsibility sits on one end of the see saw. Authority sits on the other end. In a productive, healthy environment, the seesaw balances between the two. In other words, that which the employee must accomplish as a part of the job should include the proper authority to actually get it done. And the opposite is true: for that which the employee has the

authority to accomplish, that employee should have responsibility for the outcome and results. In a toxic environment,
however, the seesaw is most often skewed, with one end sitting flat on the ground, while the other end extends straight
up into the sky, completely unbalanced.

Back in the catalog "war room," Alan no longer had any
real authority over his work. No matter what was decided as
each catalog production cycle was launched, the boss felt the
need to come in late in the game and make changes. This is
frustrating enough to any talented employee, but in this toxic
pond, Alan was still held accountable for the sales numbers
if they did not make projections, even though he had techni-
cally lost all authority over the placement of merchandise in
the catalog. After all, that was his job.

This Senior Vice President had a seasoned professional
with an entire career devoted to merchandising and selling
through catalogs on her team. She should be rejoicing that
she could turn her efforts toward other parts of the company. But she just couldn't stop changing the direction for
the team. The Toxin of Revisiting Decisions was fueled by
both her own indecision and fear, which she projected onto
Alan, and by her arrogance in her belief that she could make
a better decision than he could when his years of experience
said otherwise.

WHAT IS LEADERSHIP, ANYWAY?

Lack of clear direction from the top brass, backtrack-
ing, executing in one direction only to pull back and execute
in another, panicky knee-jerk reactions to sales dips, marketing direction change every month or every quarter.....
Do you endure any of this at your workplace? Or worse, do
you create it?

Oh, the books that have been written on Leadership! You
could sink a ship with them. Leadership qualifies as one of

the "hard to measure" aspects of life—it's difficult to put on a checklist, it's difficult to train to, it's difficult to define. One way to gauge the effectiveness (*or* destructiveness) of Leadership is to examine the environment. When the Toxin of Revisiting Decisions is poisoning the pond and the inhabitants are getting sick, then the Leadership is very poor indeed.

Why? Because real Leadership is not consistently *reactive*. Leadership forges the path and makes the way for the rest of the team to come in and perform the necessary duties. When the leaders are consistently turning around on the path to stop and re-direct, or stop and re-invent the plan, or for any other reason cease forging the path forward, then they are operating reactively.

With the beginnings of industry, the emphasis was on producing a unit of something—a plow, a boot, a sweater, a hat. Success was measured in the number of units produced at the end of the shift. "Management" was something very basic: the process of moving along a process. The end result of "good management" was a bucket full of tangible results— "stuff." The emphasis in the 1920's, 30's and 40's became studies in efficiency: what to tweak and change in order to produce more of something in a given time frame.

Frank and Lillian Gilbreth, better known for their family life portrayed in the book and movie *Cheaper by the Dozen*, were "time and motion" specialists, scientifically studying the elemental movements of tasks and creating more efficient movements. Frank had worked as an apprentice bricklayer as a young man, and took on that trade to determine whether he could minimize fatigue by reducing the number of the bricklayer's movements. He developed scaffolding that put the bricks within better reach, and ultimately increased the bricklayer's productivity by reducing the number of movements from 15 to 8 for each brick. Gilbreth is also credited for creating the rapid assembly and disassembly of rifles when servicemen are in total darkness. Frank and Lillian both focused on how to improve quality by reducing motion, critical studies for producing "stuff."

As industry increased, service businesses began to develop. Many service businesses are really "thought businesses" such as marketing, advertising, or the practice of law, whereby the "product" is made of assessments and ideas, not leather and nails. Add to this complexity the layering on of managers and other people necessary to keep the processes flowing in order to produce the end results, and an intricacy of humanity is born—the need for effective management of *people*, not processes or machines. And what is management anyway? How does it change when it involves so many people? How indeed does a leader keep everyone moving forward in the right direction, focused on the same goals, and producing to the right standards? Answering these questions became the historical beginning of the complicated topic called "business leadership." And as in all cases of effective leadership, business leadership too must start with a plan.

STRATEGY MOVES OVER FROM THE WAR DEPARTMENT

As the complexities within organizations grew, so did the ideas surrounding them. "Strategic Management" as a discipline, studied, thought about, written about, discussed in theory and in practice, emerged in the 1950's and 60's. Alfred Chandler's monumental contribution to the beginnings of this movement included his 1962 work *Strategy and Structure*, in which he concluded that organizations would be more successful if they created an overall strategy that was forward-looking. He recognized that the uncoordinated efforts of several departments within one organization and the failure to link together the function of management with the goals of the organization severely limited the organization's ability to grow and be productive. Many organizations didn't have long-term goals and weren't used to thinking past the next month's quota of items to be produced.

But it was Peter Drucker who articulated most clearly the crossing of business from *production of stuff* to what he called the *knowledge worker*—those individuals who possess the understanding, intuition, talents, and wisdom to get the job done right. Drucker authored 39 books and spent a career of five decades theorizing and thinking about humanity and management. He challenged managers and leaders to rethink the way they handled people, and consequently handled their businesses.

Drucker understood the growing complexity arising from moving into businesses constructed of ideas, and *people* who have ideas, wrapped up in the need to execute daily tasks to meet requirements to get jobs done to make a profit. Unfortunately for many employees in many environments, while Drucker understood precisely what was shifting and changing, the managers and leaders didn't (and don't) seem to understand Drucker, and so the Toxin of Revisiting Decisions continues to poison ponds everywhere today.

Every business is begun to accomplish *something*....and often it is this initial drive that counts as strategy for years within the business. But some vague sense of direction is not strategy. Many companies plug along for years without any formal strategic plan. That's easy enough to understand as the tactical plan (the daily operations) unfolds as needed, and continues to move the business forward each week, each month, each quarter. Sometimes the leaders in the organization may not fully grasp the differences between a strategic plan and a tactical plan, and become lost in the details of execution. Losing the forest for the trees, so to speak.

As mentioned earlier, real leadership is not consistently reactive. However, the business can't help but become reactive if the executives focus on the tactical plan, and lose sight of the strategic plan, or fail to build one in the first place. Instead of having a solid plan with contingencies, the business has *activities*. When the business heats up or sales dips frighten the team, these activities are replaced by *panicked* activities.

Every company and every manager will have to revisit a decision now and again. Every company that pays attention to its market, to consumer trends, and to rapidly changing technology may alter its strategic course at some point.

It is when the exception becomes the rule that the Toxin of Revisiting Decisions begins to spread its poison and infect the pond inhabitants. While leadership may be defined in a hundred ways, it surely at least encompasses the ability to maintain the strategic plan while equipping the team with the resources necessary to execute the tactical details supporting the plan. The CEO, the department head, even the middle manager must never lose sight of the overall strategic plan, or everyone stands in danger of failing to hit it.

HITTING THE WRONG TARGET DOESN'T COUNT

At the 2004 Summer Olympics in Athens, American Matthew Emmons was three points ahead in the men's 50-meter rifle target event. He had the gold sealed and no one was likely to catch him when he made a mistake that business leaders make every day—*he lost sight of his strategic plan.* He executed the *tactical* plan beautifully--when he fired his rifle it was a near perfect bulls-eye, the bullet lodged within a dime-sized space. Only it was lodged in his *neighbor's* target.

Strategy cannot be effectively accomplished without prioritization. Very simply, focusing on the wrong target is a failure to prioritize. And hitting the wrong target, even if it's a bulls-eye, just doesn't count.

In business, as in the Olympics, hitting the wrong target also doesn't count, but unfortunately, the end results can be far more devastating. Business failure always affects customers and employees and shareholders. Hitting the wrong target can mean layoffs—sending people home who may least be able to afford it. Hitting the wrong target may mean reduced benefits for the workers who need them the most. Hitting the wrong target hurts lives.

PRIORITIZATION AND STRATEGY

Up until the last century, nature generally dictated priorities. The moon determined the time to plant; livestock was born in the spring. It got dark earlier in the winter and later in the summer, and the harvest was a function of the season. In modern business complexity, there is no luxury of following nature's lead. In the list of seemingly endless tasks, knowing what to do *first* can prevent a leader from missing the target all together.

Matthew Emmons commented after the Olympics that he normally hones in on the target number, which sits above the target, and then lowers his rifle to the bulls-eye. But in Athens, he missed that first step. He just focused, and shot. That first step was rather important to his strategic plan of winning a gold medal; indeed, not knowing what to do first wrecked Matthew's strategic plan. He lost the gold on a perfect shot.

Additionally, without prioritization, a strategic plan can easily disintegrate into a to-do list. A to-do list that you hope will get accomplished, or one that if you are lucky, you'll finish, or failing that, you panic yourself or your staff into high gear and action. But hope, luck, and panic are not strategies, though many companies act as though they are.

It is a familiar complication factor that companies occasionally achieve good business results without strategy or prioritization. When this happens, it actually reinforces the idea that flying by the seat of your pants works, and the Toxin of Revisiting Decisions becomes a stronger poison in the pond.

ONE, TWO, TIE YOUR SHOE; THREE, FOUR, SHUT THE DOOR...

Sally and Ann, both marketing managers for a mid-sized software development company, laughed silently as they caught each other yawning. Sally rolled her eyes and pretended to fall asleep as the Vice President of Marketing droned on and on in the quarterly "Planning" Meeting. Oh well, at least they were coming up with an important "to-do" list, and their boss had promised this time that the list would be prioritized. Maybe now they'd have some support and resources to actually bring a marketing campaign to life.

But Sally was fuming when she met Ann for their own weekly update a few days later. She had just met with the VP, who had come from a meeting with the CEO in which he had assigned a 1-5 on each of the tasks, supposedly meaning they had an order of importance.

"So what exactly are you upset about, Sally? Isn't this what we've wanted?" asked Ann, "For the CEO to rank the projects?"

"Look at the note at the bottom," was all Sally could manage. Ann read out loud, "Here are the priorities as I see them; however, they are all important and must get done." In one sentence the CEO had done two things: wiped out the priority list that he had created, and indicated that he didn't understand what priority actually meant. Sally and Ann knew from prior experience that without prioritization, their budget would get very thin across the board. Everything on the list would get funded, but nothing would get funded well enough to work as it should. The CEO's dictate meant that Sally and Ann would both make small steps on each "to-do" and fail to do anything very well in an effort to get the entire list finished by the deadlines.

Brainstorming by definition does not lend itself to rational and ordered execution. The final ideas produced in the brainstorming session must be subjected to prioritization, *and* measured against the objectives of the strategic plan. Anything less creates an environment of ad-hoc and last minute projects. And last-minute *always* means revisiting decisions, which means the toxin spreads.

If the top executives do not believe in setting priorities and sticking to them, and they have no outside pressure to do so from a parent company, stockholders, or other, it is likely that the ad-hoc environment will continue as normal operating procedures.

THE TACTICAL NIGHTMARE

Ad-hoc decision-making creates tactical nightmares for those required to bring the decision to life. And it's generally not the senior executives who are burning their weekends chasing the chaos, up all night implementing the changes and making the revisions. They go home, often satisfied that in the last minute they made an amazing catch, a dive for the ball that worked, or a play change that will save the game. They often fail to see the toll it takes on the ones left behind to execute it.

Reactive decisions are most often the product of haste. After-hours Blackberry "conversations" make it easy to alter the entire course of a project with a few keystrokes. But what feels urgent and important at 10:30 pm on a Wednesday night will still be urgent and important in the morning, with the appropriate stakeholders present to make a reasoned decision. This propensity to make quick decisions without the proper stakeholders can lead to disastrous consequences.

In a swift reaction to a consumer sales dip and negative feedback about pricing, the CEO and COO made an "after hours" Blackberry decision to lower the prices of three products to move them more quickly. But the merchandising manager could not be reached for input because she was at her niece's school play. The situation felt urgent and the top two executives made the decision and called in the IT team to execute the changes on the web. The new pricing announcement was posted at 12:01 a.m.

They briefly considered delaying until the morning when they could consult the inventory reports and the manager's judgment, but the Toxin of Revisiting Decisions is not only poisonous, but impatient, and cannot bear waiting. So the decision was made in the dark of night when everything feels more urgent than it truly is.

The morning's sunlight brought bad news. The inventory levels wouldn't support a sale on these particular items, and they couldn't be reordered fast enough to prevent a stock-out. As a result of revisiting the decision on the pricing of these few items, customer relations was actually further damaged, not helped, as orders went unfilled and customers hit the roof. "Why on earth would you promote something like this when you don't have enough of it?" was the most commonly received question in the very busy customer service center over the next few days. Additionally, the CEO was furious with the merchandising manager for not being available when the decision was made. "I only made the best decision I could with the information that was communicated to me," he railed, shifting the blame for the failed situation away from his impatience and onto her after-hours unavailability.

Every project needs some degree of passion to be fulfilled to its best expression. Unfortunately, in an environment filled with the Toxin of Revisiting Decisions, the passion becomes centered around the negatives, the lacks, the disgruntled and huddled masses who have no leadership and feel trampled upon. The passion fuels the negativity, not the positive achievement of the team working in unison to achieve the company's objective and celebrate.

WHY IT MATTERS

Alan, Sarah, Sally and Ann are all real people in real companies, all growing sick from the Toxin of Revisiting Decisions. When employees continually have their work dismissed, changed, or undone, it fosters an atmosphere of detachment and fear. Rather than invest themselves emotionally in their work, employees pull back, unwilling to watch their hard work get flushed down the toilet, especially again and again.

"I'll just do my job and keep my head down" becomes the dull mantra. Talented employees will start looking for work elsewhere, and those who can't leave—maybe they need the benefits, maybe they can't risk looking, etc—those employees will stop pouring passion into their work. Ultimately the business will lose good people; the good people who execute the tactical plans that keep the business moving forward.

One thing is certain, if the Toxin of Revisiting Decisions remains unchecked, the business will suffer, and the pond will grow sick.

TO LEARN HOW TO REMOVE DEADLY TOXIN 6: REVISITING DECISIONS FROM YOUR WORKPLACE, READ CLEAN UP 4: EXERCISE CREATIVE DISCIPLINE.

Deadly Toxin 6 Poison Control:
Are you revisiting decisions?
Your particular circumstances may not resemble the ones discussed here, but surely there are ways to improve your pond. Answer these two questions to explore ways your pond may be toxic. If you are very brave, have your staff answer them as well!

1. How frequently do you change the course of a project after the initial timeline has been set?

2. What measures can you take in your area at work to ensure that projects are clearly defined and meet company objectives from the beginning to avoid revisiting decisions during the development process?

Deadly Toxin 7: Living the Lie

Knowledge is proud that it knows so much;wisdom is humble that it knows no more.

--William Cowper

The devastating phone call came at 7:30 pm. Even the way the phone rang seemed to scream disaster. The voice on the other end only confirmed it. "Steve, Lisa, we need you to come in first thing in the morning for more tests. The tumor is malignant, but we're going to put together the right plan in the morning. Okay? You still with me? First thing tomorrow, we tackle this head on."

"Am I going to die?" Steve whispered into phone, so afraid that covering his fear in false bravado never even occurred to him. Lisa took in a sharp breath, and squeezed his arm, while squeezing back her own tears.

"Not if I have anything to do with it," said the strong voice on the phone. "We'll put together the plan in the morning, and we're going to beat this thing. Now try to get some rest tonight. I know it'll be hard, but you need to rest."

Steve dropped the phone, unable to even put it back in its cradle, and sagged onto the couch. He looked at his wife of fifteen years, mother of his children, and companion in life. He never needed her before as much as he did now—if only to comfort him and tell him it was going to be okay, even if it was a lie.

Lisa sat beside him and wrapped her arms around his large frame. "It's going to be okay," she said. "Whatever it is, we're in it together, and we will face it together." Steve sighed with relief. Just to hear her say it out loud gave him courage.

They sat together quietly on the couch for awhile, each one absorbed with too much emotion to speak. Finally, Lisa said, "I need to call Dorothy and let her know I won't be coming in tomorrow." She got up off the couch to make the call.

Lisa is a highly successful executive in a fast growing marketing and public relations company. She has been with the founder from the near beginning of the venture, when fortune and fame and expensive evening gowns were still a far-off dream. They were swimming in success now, and Lisa directed all of the communications for the company. She loved her job, though the environment was not always a healthy one. She'd had a few run in's with the founder, who was also the CEO, over taking vacation and being with her family during times the CEO considered "awkward" for the business.

Lisa picked up the phone and called Dorothy at home. "Dorothy, the tests came back today, and we just got off the phone with the doctor. The tumor is….." she stumbled, not able to bring herself to say the "C" word, "…very bad. I won't be in tomorrow."

There was a long pause. Lisa thought at first the connection had been lost. "Dorothy?" she asked, just to check.

"I'm here, Lisa. Listen, I'm *really* sorry about that. Truly I am. Steve is a great guy. But you know we are right in the middle of a new launch campaign with this client, and the communications plan isn't finished, and it is vital to the success of this launch." Dorothy left the sentence hanging there, clearly expecting Lisa to jump in and assure her that no matter what the circumstances, she'd get the plan finished on time.

"Dorothy, did you even *hear* me?" asked Lisa, stunned at her boss' response to the most tragic news she'd ever received.

"Of course I *heard* you, Lisa," said Dorothy. There was a very long and painful pause as Dorothy waited for Lisa to volunteer to pick up the slack over the weekend, and Lisa waited for Dorothy to get a heart.

Finally, Dorothy grudgingly said, "Fine. But when you get in on Monday, there's going to be a helluva lot of work to do."

TELLTALE TOXIC SIGNS

Lisa knew Dorothy was annoyed when her high-level employees took time off. After all, if *she* were this dedicated to the success of the company, then so should they be. But Lisa had managed to live with it, and work her family's schedule around the job so they got to spend time together vacationing. Lisa did work very long hours, though, and felt entitled to the vacation time specified in her employment contract. It's not like she was asking for something that wasn't already hers.

But it never occurred to Lisa that Dorothy would have the same response to her scary news, as if she were saying "I know you are swamped at the office and projects are undone, but I am abandoning you to head for the coast this weekend." Lisa did not know that she was suffering from the Toxin of Living the Lie, and this poison had been spreading through the pond for many years.

The Toxin of Living the Lie is the most dangerous of all the Seven Deadly Toxins. It creeps about, cloaked as a wolf in sheep's clothing, ready to pounce in situations where the victims are most vulnerable, and most unprepared for the assault.

A TREE IS KNOWN BY ITS FRUIT

Ranging from the absurdly inhuman, as in the true story above, to everyday slips, leaders spread the Toxin of Living the Lie when they believe themselves to possess excellent and admirable character traits, but in reality possess and exhibit quite the opposite. A deep chasm exists between who they think they are, and who they actually are. These leaders often live their entire lives defending their own point of view, largely in an effort to avoid coming to terms with the chasm.

The Bible is full of obvious statements, as often the most profound truths of the universe are the most simple. This principle is no exception as Jesus tells his disciples, "A tree is known by its fruit." How simple! How profound! There is no trickery possible here.

A crabapple tree can call itself a peach tree all day long, believe itself to be a peach tree, talk to others about the glorious peaches it produces every season, but that crabapple tree will be found false when the fruit is borne. There is a time and a season when the ugly truth exposes the deep chasm.

When this happens, it can be devastating for the employees involved, largely because the Toxin of Living the Lie can rarely exist without a sense of betrayal. Feeling betrayed ranks among the deepest of all unbearable human emotions. When employees invest emotionally in a company or cause that they feel passionate about, and are emotionally connected to a leader they feel is a powerful embodiment of the organization's passion, the fall from the top can be very painful indeed.

Lisa knew that Dorothy had "issues" with several things, ranging from Lisa's desire to take off normal time to spend with her family to being irritated that no one seemed to "care" about the business as much as she did. In Dorothy's mind, everyone who worked for her should be willing to sacrifice for the company the way she did.

But Lisa truly never saw *this* betrayal coming. After all of her service to the company, her devotion, and her passion, how could Dorothy abandon her like this in her time of need? What Lisa never knew was that Dorothy was never concerned about her and Steve, or anyone or anything other than her own selfish pursuits. This is the chasm between who Dorothy thinks she is, and who she actually is. And because she has believed herself to be honorable, giving, kind, and even spiritual, Dorothy has projected that image to those around her whenever possible. She has been a crabapple tree promising the glorious peach harvest to come. What Lisa is experiencing is the undeniable fruit-bearing season of the crabapple tree, and she is astonished to discover that peaches are nowhere to be found. This simple truth exposes the chasm.

When Melanie Smith's mother fell ill and had to be hospitalized, she was forthright with her Human Resources Department. "I need to take off three days to be with my mom," she'd said, not even really asking because she assumed it would be fine. After all, she was personally responsible for $72 million in sales *in one year* for this large fabric manufacturer, and had established herself as a world-class salesperson and account representative. She was also an impeccable decorator, and used her skill to gain admittance into the largest hotel chains in the country and supply all their fabric needs, which were, of course, substantial. She naturally assumed that her request would be easily accommodated.

When the HR Director told her in reply that she couldn't have the time off because it was December, and the company had a 25-year policy that no one took time off in December, Melanie almost didn't know how to react. "Did you hear me say my mother is in the hospital?" she asked. Of course she'd heard. Since Melanie is forthright in her dealings with others, she then said, "You are forcing me into the position of taking my sick days to take care of my mother, and I am very uncomfortable with that." That is of course a common practice among employees in numerous companies when their lives need extra attention. And who can blame them when a family member's health is on the line? Melanie went to be with her mother, and called in sick for three days. On day three, the HR Director stated, "You will need to bring back your mother's hospital bracelet in order not to be penalized for this time." Melanie was aghast. Truly aghast. She envisioned that they wanted her to rip the very bracelet from her mother's wrist, since she had endured complications and heavy bleeding from the surgery, and the doctor wouldn't release her yet. "So sorry, mom, I know you need this, but I need it more!"

When Melanie returned to work, she did indeed bring a copy of her mother's hospital bracelet...along with her resignation letter. And another business lost a great talent because of a Toxin in the pond.

The owner of the company called Melanie in a panic. "You are the best design rep we have. I can't let you quit! I'll fly down and straighten things out." He meant he'd fly down from Aspen, where he was skiing with his family, on vacation, despite the 25-year policy. The Toxin of Living the Lie was exposed. Melanie moved on to another company, and never looked back.

SAY ONE THING, DO ANOTHER

The Toxin of Living the Lie does not always produce such dramatic situations. There are many everyday circumstances in which the Toxin erodes the health of the workplace, and spreads its poison.

In Ginny Smith's sales company, the senior management seemed to really care about the workforce, and would spend thousands of dollars each year on employee surveys to gather feedback on everything from the cafeteria food to the benefits plan. At the annual company picnic and business review, the leaders would announce that they'd "heard" the workforce, and this or that thing would be addressed.

Then things would continue on, business as usual, because the mid-management level in the chain of command wouldn't implement the changes. The Senior Team didn't follow up, and didn't seem to notice that the great announcements had dwindled into nothingness.

People are generally patient and willing to forgive, at least at first. After all, the company is busy with many things, and maybe the plans hit a snag. But there was a bit more cynicism when the surveys came around the second year. "Why do it again? Nothing happened last time.....," grumbled the employees. The great announcements were made at the annual picnic/business review, but once again dwindled into nothing. When the surveys came around in year three, they were a company joke. Nobody believed anything different would happen, and lost faith in the process, the company, and the leadership.

When surveyed, most managers think they are doing a great job managing their employees. But their employees often have a different perspective. According to a survey of 1,854 U.S. workers conducted by Rasmussen Reports LLC for Hudson Firm, 92% of managers say they're doing an "excellent" or "good" job managing their employees, but only 67% of workers agree with them. The gap between how these managers rate themselves and how their employees rate them demonstrates the chasm between who these managers are, and who they think they are.

The gap produces negative results for the company, including turnover and less motivated employees. When employees are inspired by their leaders, they pour more of their own passion into their work. When they are betrayed by them, they pull back, disengage, and often find a way to leave for another pond.

An obvious way to address the gap would be to incorporate more employee-based feedback. The popularity of the 360-degree review process indicates that some companies use these methods. However, the individual being reviewed often gets to choose the staff members above and below that will perform the review. Really, how much honesty can truly be expected? Employees are afraid that the manager will be able to determine where the negative comments have come from, and endure bad consequences.

And often, the real problems are at the very top of the organization, with the senior team and the CEO. How many CEO's are really interested in hearing honest negative feedback from their staff members? Next to none. The Hudson Firm study said that only just 26% of the workers surveyed said their company even *allows* them to take part in evaluations of the higher-ups. The Toxin of Living the Lie has no interest in being exposed.

AVOIDING MIRRORS

Confronting one's own short-comings is never an easy task, but among those infected with the Toxin of Living the Lie it is practically unheard of. That's part of the reason the Toxin continues to spread. Those individuals who do summon the courage to confront the leader in an organization often find themselves summarily fired, or re-assigned to "special projects"--always a death-sentence to a career.

Sometimes, the leader will solicit feedback, especially if they have a spiritual side. After all, confessing our sins and attempting to do better is the Christian credo, and at least a part of being a wise and seasoned leader, right? The real question is whether or not the individual is truly interested in the answers.

Those leaders who spread the Toxin of Living the Lie cannot bear to face their own shortcomings, and will simply find a way to deny the truth. If they never look in the mirror, then their appearance can be whatever they desire it to be. The crabapple tree will never see their own crabapples. Though saying they are receptive to the feedback in the beginning, this leader will find a way to subvert it, re-direct it, or turn it on the very person they asked. One thing is sure—they will not accept it.

Adam Johnson had negotiated a million dollar annual base salary, and was proud of it. He felt he deserved it, even though the company was suffering financially, and had taken a downward turn over the last 18 months. True, he had inherited some significant problems, but had failed to turn anything around to a positive in his year and a half tenure. He decided, with the board's approval, that the company would experience its first RIF (reduction in force; layoff) in its 50-year history. He called together all of his Vice Presidents, and told them to cut 20% of their department budget in staff reductions.

The Vice Presidents dutifully identified those individuals whose lives would forever change the day they showed up for work and were escorted out of the building, never to return. They dutifully submitted their lists, and dutifully fulfilled their obligation on that fateful day. The Vice Presidents sent home a 63-year old woman who didn't make more than $43,000, along with scores of family wage earners barely meeting the country's median income. The company moved on, though the financials did not improve. Adam continued to praise the team for handling the difficulties so well, and thanked God whenever possible for such a great opportunity to lead such a wonderful company.

Six months after the RIF, Adam Johnson gave his two primary senior team members—the COO and the CMO—raises of $100,000 each. After all, they were significantly behind him in their earning scale, and carried the weight of the company along with him. They deserved to be fully compensated for their efforts. And at $225,000 each, Adam thought they just weren't taking home what they deserved. A solid $325,000 and a bonus sounded more suitable, and also made him feel much better about the distance between their paychecks and his.

It never even occurred to him that anyone on the staff would read the public records posted every quarter by the company on the Internet to see what he had done. Beyond that, he didn't feel he had done anything wrong. They *deserved* that money.

Is it any wonder that a Harris Poll conducted in 2004 revealed that as low as 28% percent of workers feel that their top leaders show integrity and morality?

The poison of Living the Lie doesn't always manifest itself so dramatically. In hundreds of ways every work week, every leader living in the chasm between who they think they are and who they really are is eroding the day-to-day confidence of their employees. The Vice President who loudly talks about the sermons heard at church on Sunday and his duties as a deacon lives in the chasm when he takes credit for an idea in front of the CEO that one of his subordinates came up with. The Director who fails to mention the employee who stayed up all night preparing his report, as he delivers it to his boss, also lives in the chasm.

THE IVORY TOWER AND CLASS DIVISION

Scott Stevens had boundless energy and a choirboy aura. He had an impressive record, at least from school, graduating #1 in his MBA class from the prestigious Wharton School of Business. His track record hadn't quite lived up to that initial promise, but now he knew he'd have his chance to shine as new CEO to a hardware and auto parts company. He embraced his new job with enthusiasm, and why shouldn't he? He had just landed a million dollar salary, with a great bonus plan on top of that! He was elated that his talent level was finally recognized.

Scott was having a great time running his new company. He knew he should spend more time out and around the office, getting to know the staff. After all, that's what good CEO's do, right? But he never had anything to really say to anybody, and he could feel the stiff silence at the last company meeting as he talked about his daughters' private school and his gated community. He really just couldn't relate to most of his employees.

One day Scott had spent some time studying a survey on the company's customer demographics. Much of the data surprised him, and it was on his mind quite a bit.

When he ran into Sheila Edwards in the hallway, a staff-level member who had been working on a project through his office and with whom he struck a friendship, he blurted out, "Sheila, did you know the average household income of our customers is $45,000 per year? How does ANYONE live on $45,000 per year?" He blathered on a little while longer about how impossible that seemed to him, and then went on his way. He didn't know that Sheila earned just barely $40,000 per year, and the 200 workers in his distribution center earned well under that. Sheila just shook her head and walked on down the hall.

Can a CEO that out of touch with his customer truly be effective? Can a CEO that out of touch with his work force know anything about what they desire or need?

According to a study conducted by the Institute for Policy Studies titled "Executive Excess 2006, the 13th Annual CEO Compensation Survey" (found on www.faireconomy.org), CEO's in 1980 made 42 times what their average employee made. In simple terms, if the average employee made $15,000, the CEO made $630,000. That's a significant spread when put in simple dollar terms. However, that was 1980. In 2005, average CEO's made 411 times what their average employee made. To demonstrate, that means if the average employee made $30,000, the CEO made $12,330,000. Of course, much of this income is "hidden" in bonuses, stock awards, payouts such as returns on insurance co-pays, or car allowances and gas cards, or country club memberships. The CEO can stand up in front of his employees and deny that his "base" pay is excessive, while still bringing home the benefits of a $12 million dollar package *annually*.

Strikingly, average salaries across the board for American workers have increased barely 5% over the last 16 years, but CEO pay has risen 300% in the same timeframe. How is this possible? Their rate of pay has far exceeded the rate of growth of profits for their companies. What this means is that CEO's take home a much larger percentage of the company's profit line, leaving less for operating capital, employee benefits, and shareholder dividends. Can a CEO whose package includes reimbursement for doctor's office co-pays really understand what it means to the Distribution Center worker whose wife needs exploratory heart surgery, but simply cannot afford the $1000 deductible? And since his company cut the benefits package, all "non-emergency" surgeries have an additional $500 deductible. That $1500, up front, in cash, may as well be half a million dollars to this family. Meanwhile, the CEO's family gets reimbursed for all prescriptions, co-pays, and even their kids get their braces covered as a standard part of the package.

If worker pay had increased over the last 16 years at the same rate as CEO pay, then this distribution worker would be making over $110,000 instead of a mere $30,000. And if the minimum wage amount had grown at the same rate as CEO pay, it would have been $22.61 in 2005 instead of $5.15. How can these CEO's possibly understand the needs of their customers or the needs of their employees when their own lifestyles are so far removed they can't even relate on any common plane? The discrepancy in lifestyles is enough to spread the Toxin of Living the Lie, as the leaders at the top have no understanding as to what it means to face a doctor's bill that cannot be paid, or further education for the children that cannot be secured.

If a pay ratio of 411:1 is unfair, as nearly *everyone* except those on the 411 side of the ratio do feel, then what is fair? Interestingly, J.P. Morgan, over 100 years ago, advocated that the ratio between CEO's and employees should never exceed 20:1. And Peter Drucker, the father of management theory, agreed with this ratio, writing about it in 1982. Until his death in 2004, he stood by his statements, believing that the enormity of CEO pay caused the CEO to ask the wrong questions, and ultimately, rewarded the executive for doing the self-serving thing, rather than the right thing.

But even worse, when the CEO fails and is given the boot by the board, shareholders, customers or the public, he gets a pay *raise*. The severance packages paid out over the last year represent staggering amounts of money awarded for failure. When a fired CEO leaves his post with $40,000,000, box seats to his favorite ball team, use of a luxury corporate apartment, and even administrative staff workers, he is literally stealing from the employees who remain behind, doing the work that keeps the company alive.

WHY IT MATTERS

Leadership starts at the top, and the form that leadership takes will shape the company, its programs, its marketing, its benefits package for employees, and nearly everything about the corporation. *Ethics* simply means the guiding principles that govern a person's behavior. When the leaders are perceived by their employees as ruthless for their own success, lacking in integrity, self-serving, and disconnected from the realities of the business, or even what it takes to raise a family in America, the Toxin of Living the Lie is in full swing. These leaders rarely, if ever, perceive themselves this way, thus perpetuating the chasm, and continuing to work and function within, to the detriment of their companies and employees.

TO LEARN HOW TO REMOVE DEADLY TOXIN 7: LIVING THE LIE FROM YOUR WORKPLACE, READ CLEAN UP 5: GAIN HUMILITY.

Deadly Toxin 7 Poison Control:
Are you living the lie?
Your particular circumstances may not resemble the ones discussed here, but surely there are ways to improve your pond. Answer these two questions to explore ways your pond may be toxic. If you are very brave, have your staff answer them as well!

1. List any situations in your company where you have observed the Toxin of Living the Lie at work. What role did you play, if any, in these situations?

2. Do you know your company's policies on time off for staff, including vacation, personal days and emergency time off? Do you know what your company policies are for the lowest paid workers in your company? How do they measure up against the policies for the highest paid employees?

PART

2

Let's Clean It Up

Clean Up Method 1: Commit to the Process

Management is about People.

--Peter Drucker

Management is *not* foremost about the task at hand. It's not about telling people what to do, or simply delegating and ensuring tasks are complete, or enjoying executive perks. It's not about solo effort and heroic saves. It's certainly not about exercising the ego or building an empire at the expense of everyone else on the team.

Management is **coordinating the work of a group of people to achieve the organization's goals**. Good management inspires, motivates, and taps into the passion available only to humanity. Good management provides opportunity for employees to flourish, and understands how to apply it appropriately in the organization to existing problems. Application of natural talent to specific problems moves the business forward better than any strategy or process. Good management increases morale, loyalty, commitment and ultimately, productivity and profits.

But *Deadly Toxin 1: Stifling Talent* poisons the pond and prevents good management from occurring. The Toxin of Stifling Talent only recognizes the "mechanics" of job function. In a toxic environment, the manager only focuses on the task at hand, and completely misses the beauty and power of working with people to solve business problems.

The Toxin of Stifling Talent can be reduced and eliminated by leaders and managers who are willing to **Commit to the Process**. This clean up involves understanding what it means to manage *people*, to grasp the core of being human. Committing to the Process means understanding that because employees *are* human, they are bound to certain limitations and restrictions. Conversely, excellent benefits come built right into the employee, if the leaders would only leverage them. As noted in Part I, employees *are individual bundles of energy, motivation, compassion, and desire for achievement. They are a mix of every experience of their upbringing and education, of their interactions and gene pool.* This uncontrived, uncontrollable mix is the bonus that can produce amazing results for the manager and the company who commits to the process, and provides a pond for talent to flourish. No machine can be motivated by passion to solve a problem like a human being.

THE HURRIED EXECUTIVE

The higher ranks of management are often populated by individuals who propelled themselves forward at a lightning speed pace, or by those able to accomplish large amounts of work in small amounts of time, earning promotions as they go. As discussed in Part 1, the qualities that make a person a stellar individual performer do not necessarily equip them for the tasks of managing people. Executives are especially responsible, not just for managing their own staff, but for setting the tone and philosophy for the entire organization. The path the executives forge *will be* the path for the whole organization, just as the body is led by the head.

If a manager continues to rely on his own stellar performance pace and self-sufficiency, he will find it difficult not to stifle the talent in the staff he is managing. Just because a manager *can* accomplish a task doesn't mean he *should*. Leadership is in part the *development* of talented staff, in order to equip the company to move into the future. It's easy to lose sight of this if you are an effective solo worker who has now become a manager.

Additionally, all managers can falter in leadership if they can't slow down enough to allow for the humanity of their staff to regulate the flow of information and activity. Committing to the Process means understanding that this slow down is necessary when additional people are involved in the work.

A properly managed course of business activity will reap far greater rewards and profits than a hurried, impatient flow. In fact, a hurried, impatient flow exists in business for only two reasons: either to satisfy somebody's ego, or to hide poor management.

Additionally, entrepreneurs can struggle with the leap from initiating an idea to growing it into a company simply because they can no longer control the form, function or flow of information and activity. The required "slow down" in pace can breed frustration for the owner who refuses to acknowledge a slow down is necessary.

"Increasing top line revenue" can be a great excuse for requiring a hurried, impatient flow. Every leader should feel the responsibility to increase top line revenue and help their company grow. But top line revenue says less about the company's stability and sustainability than bottom line profits. Top line revenue may exceed $10 million dollars, but if your expenses eat your margin and you end up *spending* $10 million and one penny, then you're moving backwards, not forwards. You've gained nothing.

CLARITY IS CRITICAL

The larger the organization, the more people each decision must flow through in order to be properly executed. This necessarily requires *more time*. As the process for completion of the project makes its way through the management chain, there is also more opportunity for misinterpretation and error. As information or instructions move along the chain from the CEO to the VP to the manager to the staff person executing the task, opportunities for distortion are created. Remember the telephone game? The words are clearly spoken by the originator, but as each individual hears what they hear then passes it on, each 'hearer' has a chance to get it wrong, even introducing various agendas and opinions, further distorting the message.

When there is more than one person thinking, creating vision, and executing tasks to fulfill the vision, as is the case in nearly every business in America, *clarity of that vision* becomes even more critical. How can something not understood be passed on? How can something not crystallized be acted upon?

The managers and staff must have an understanding of the overall goals of the organization and an understanding of how the completion of their tasks fits into achieving those goals. That sounds like basic management, doesn't it? It is astounding how many companies operate without this principle in play. Everyone may have a rudimentary, fuzzy understanding of the company's goals, just enough information not to fail. But not failing isn't the same as winning.

By understanding vision, goals, and brand offering clearly, each manager has a better opportunity to make sure the tasks they are responsible for conform to the overall vision. Mistakes or miscommunications will likely surface on their own, as everyone is clear about what they should be doing, and what they shouldn't be doing. Without this understanding, wrong interpretations are likely to abound. No one intends to adopt a strategy that wastes time and company resources. No leader begins the day by saying, "Today we are going to waste our resources, and be ineffective by spending half our day on projects we aren't even responsible for, and fail to give proper attention to any projects which would actually move the business forward." Yet this happens every day at thousands of businesses across the country.

Committing to the process means understanding who you are. If you cannot articulate your company's reason for existence, its persona, and the value of your brand offering, then lock your senior team in a room and hammer it out until you can. Once the senior team is clear, the goal should be to have everyone in the building able to repeat the foundational principles of the company, and the guiding vision. Really, if you don't know what it is, how will your employees? And if nobody knows what it is, how can anyone measure whether or not it's being followed?

Michael Dell is committed to clarity for his management team and every employee. Each quarter, the executives pass on to the managers the top five goals, and identify which of the top five is the top *one*. Posters are made and hung in the buildings. The top five and the top one of five are re-iterated at meetings. Every manager of every department knows how their work fits into the overall strategy to achieve these goals. The very same goals come up every morning on every computer screen in the company, ensuring unity and cohesion of effort *from every employee*. How many people in your organization can even recite the brand statement, let alone the strategic goals for the quarter? Do you even have strategic goals for the quarter, or is all the activity a reaction to some movement in the business?

Committing to the Process means understanding the importance of vision for the entire team, from the top of the organization down to the very bottom rung, and empowering the appropriately talented employees to do the job to reach the vision.

Google's employees proudly spout out their mission, which clearly elevates the everyday tactical work to a higher plane for all of them. Their mission is "to organize the world's information and make it universally accessible and useful." This statement, along with the rest of Google's foundational statements, form a lens of clarity through which all employees can judge their work. How does your pond compare?

CUSTOMERS COUNT, WHY DON'T EMPLOYEES?

Companies go to great efforts today to study the demographics of their customers and speak to them with excellent products and customer service, answering their personalized needs. Developing loyalty programs, customer-centric promotions, and other brand campaigns all presume that connecting with the customer will produce better results for the company. Rewarding consistent customers with airline miles, cash back, free meals and entertainment have become standards, along with the old-school rewards catalog of electronics, grills and outdoor equipment. Though experts may debate whether or not these programs actually increase the dollars spent at any individual outfit, the cultural expectation is now cemented: "what *else* is in it for me" is the customer's first question when considering a purchase. Some have commented that loyalty programs are now the "price of doing business."

Should anyone be surprised that this cultural shift is also occurring at the workplace for employees? Certainly *not*, when the demographic data of Generation Xers and Millenniums are added into the equation. The upcoming employee ranks see the world as existing to provide prosperity and fun for them. This is not to say that they don't work hard— they absolutely do. But they work *differently*, with different motivations and expectations about everything, including the workplace. Every company would do well to understand that the principles that generate a loyal customer are some of the same principles that generate a loyal *employee*. When a company taps into the human component of the employee, and answers for them the question "what *else* is in it for me?" they stand to acquire and retain the highest talent.

Talent is the untapped potential to unleash at your workplace. It's not so difficult to find employees who can answer a job description and fill a role. But don't you want your employees to climb mountains for you and the company objectives? Don't you want unparalleled employee loyalty? Well, guess what--you don't get it by demanding it. But you can get it by committing to the process, understanding what truly motivates talented individuals and providing it in your pond. You will be glad you did.

Employment at your company is a part of your brand statement. Word of mouth advertising starts in your building, for both your product, and the experience of working for you.

In the 1980's, EDS was known as the company that delivered solid business computer solutions, but was a terrible place to work, with long hours and little pay. Management's attitude toward the workforce dictated that everyone at EDS should be grateful to have a job with such a fabulous company. This alone should satisfy the employee's needs. No workplace can afford this attitude any longer.

In some cases the employment environment can even ruin the product reputation. When customers learn that employees suffered in misery while making the product, they will refuse to buy it--consider all of the products tainted by accusations of child labor in third world countries.

Of course, the company's employment brand statement can also be stunningly positive. This does not happen by accident. This only happens at companies where the leadership is committed to the process, clarifies vision, and puts resources into caring for employees. Patagonia, the west coast producers of outdoor clothing and gear, receives over 900 resumes for every one job opening they have, with very little turnover even making a position available. Patagonia has clearly committed to the process of caring for employees. With extraordinary focus on meeting the employee's deepest needs and passions, Patagonia offers all employees two months paid leave to work with the charity of their choice, a nearly unimaginable opportunity for most people. The company was also one of the first in the country to establish an onsite daycare, thus relieving anxious parents of the great burden of worrying about their child's safety and well-being. A quick trot across the parking lot puts any issues to rest.

The Container Store also consistently ranks among the top places to work. With much higher pay than the average retail store worker, and extensive training opportunities, The Container Store has steadily built an amazingly dedicated employee base with low turnover rates, which hover around 10% in an industry that averages 100% yearly.

Kip Tindell, founder and CEO of the successful chain, has a simple philosophy when it comes to employees: put them first, even before the customers. "If you take care of your employees," he says, "they will take care of your customers, and that will take care of your shareholders."

"As an employer," he continues, "I feel we have a moral obligation to create an environment that employees are excited about getting up out of bed and coming to each day — an environment where they can thrive in their career, make an impact on the company's future and where they're surrounded by other great people."

Does it matter? Yes! The Container Store sales have grown an average of 15 percent to 20 percent a year since it started in Dallas in 1978.

Employment at your company has a brand identity too—would you cringe to know what it is? Or worse, deny it? The brand identity of employment at your company is what the majority of your employees say it is. Are you listening?

IT TAKES TIME TO BUILD

Graniterock has been a family-owned quarry business since 1900, and currently employs over 700 people in 18 locations across California.

Begun before the turn of the century, this family-built, family-owned, and family-loved company had been successful for a very long time. But when CEO Bruce Woolpert heard a comment from one of his managers at a company celebration, he took it to heart. The manager, commenting on the company's successful past, was speculating about the future. He remarked, "I wonder if we're doing the things necessary to take the company forward into the *next* 85 years."

Woolpert thought long and hard about that question, and decided that no, they weren't doing the things necessary to be successful going forward. In fact, he decided that his company had developed just like too many other run-of-the-mill corporations, and some very important things needed to change. Woolpert might be like hundreds of other CEO's who have a startling moment of clarity and decide to initiate change in their organizations. Only he actually took the action necessary and stuck to it to change the current climate and culture. Woolpert *committed to the process*, and made some foundational changes.

At the time of the conversation, the company had two Vice Presidents in charge of approving nearly every decision within the company, including what kind of hubcaps to buy for the trucks. The staff wouldn't make any sort of decision without the green light from the executives. Woolpert recognized this sort of centralization of power was demoralizing to a staff that could certainly be empowered to do more on their own. He also knew that it would take more than a company meeting championing the new ideas for the culture to actually change.

"It took us about six years before we had really strong self-leadership," Woolpert says. "A lot of it is building trust, letting people know this is not a trick, this is real." In the many years it took Graniterock to reinforce the new culture, the employees have gained empowerment, self-trust, and an increased passion to see *their* company succeed. Employees used to be assigned to the few training classes the company offered. Now, they create their own professional development plans and take a multitude of company-sponsored classes to meet their goals. Additionally, employees have been empowered not just to perform their jobs, but to make them better. Since the change, Graniterock has won a multitude of industry, community and national awards lauding its practices. Woolpert believes it is simply because the company now has over 700 improvement specialists at work for the company: each of its employees.

Graniterock has successfully created a pond in which the inhabitants can thrive, free to exercise their best talents and focus on moving the business forward. Graniterock employees are invested in their futures in a way they weren't before, even though they may have enjoyed their job at the company. And it pays off in bottom line increases—Graniterock's complaint costs are less than .02% of sales compared to an industry average of 2%. Improved safety cuts their insurance costs. Better customer service increases customer retention, which leads to more sales. Increased morale, increased loyalty, and the passion that talented workers bring to the workplace to creatively solve problems has made Graniterock more successful than it would have been had Bruce Woolpert not committed to the process on that celebration day.

YOU CANNOT FAKE AUTHENTICITY

Understanding what motivates an employee to toil passionately for their employer is easy to explain in a book, easy for a manager to read and get fired up over, but hard to actually implement. Committing to the process is not like signing up for a new gym membership on January 1st, going three times, and never darkening the doorway again. Committing to the Process takes dedication, passion, and the ability to build relationships. This is precisely why it so often *doesn't* happen, or why it might be championed one quarter and forgotten the next. Be careful! Because your employees will know the difference. As in all things important, you cannot fake authentic commitment.

Committing to the process means understanding that employees are not workaholics, even if their managers are. It means understanding that employees have important lives outside their work commitments, and that the importance of their lives gets to be assigned by them, not their boss. A boss without children may decide that one employee's baby gets sick too often. Or that a pet dilemma is not her problem. Or that an aged parent can be someone else's responsibility. Or that a nephew's football game doesn't qualify on the same level as a "family" commitment---or, or, or. The truth is that the employee, and the employee alone, gets to decide what is important in her life, and that the boss will get much better, faster and more passionate production from everyone if they allow individuals to take care of their life's passions.

RECOGNIZING TALENT

It is impossible to foster talent if it can't be recognized to start with, but this is no easy task. Many employees look great on paper and interview beautifully. One company leader, after hiring a great "paper and interview" employee and then firing her nine months later, commented, "As I looked at the resume again after firing this individual, I thought to myself, I would hire *this* person again."

There is no shame in hiring the wrong person. The shame comes in *keeping* the wrong person past the time the poor fit is discovered. Spending time and resources attempting to mold the employee into the job can be a reckless endeavor, as other employees generally suffer for the poor fit. Compensations are made for the sub-par performer, reporting structures are twisted to work around the personality, and work is off-loaded onto other employee's because he can't or won't do it well. Making a clean break as soon as possible is the only way to minimize the impact on the other employees.

Frankly, you can administer personality tests, profile tests, job knowledge tests, require interviews from everyone from the receptionist to the CEO and still occasionally make a bad hire. Some things just don't show up for awhile. Some managers "manage" their bosses much better than their reporting staff. It might take time for a leader to see the whole picture. But once it's plain, you must take action, or risk losing the talented people by keeping the marginal one.

So what is talent? It's very narrowly thought of today in terms of performers—sports figures, singers or actors, those whom we think of as ultra-talented. But talent is present in every individual in various forms and degrees. And those talents are uniquely filtered through their personality, upbringing, experience, and work ethic. Talent is a *natural skill* or *aptitude*, a native ability that can be developed. Talent cannot be transplanted from one individual to another. But when it is present, it can be cultivated with opportunity, training, and experience. Talented individuals themselves often overlook their own abilities, because when something comes easily, it's difficult to recognize it as noteworthy. Like a fish in water, the individual may not realize that breathing oxygen through gills is something special.

The primary task of a good manager is to identify every employee's talent, and match the job needing to be done with the appropriate person. Talent also abounds at all pay scale levels. No matter what the job, there is an employee who is most suited for it, not just in terms of mechanical processes, but also in those difficult to define aspects of *talent*: the ability to motivate and inspire the team, the ability to problem solve and think proactively, the ability to prevent disaster and move the business forward.

For some leaders, admitting that there are many people who are smarter than they are, and who can accomplish the tasks better than they can is more difficult than scaling Everest. When the ego is involved and agitated, the obvious answer gets buried under personal agendas and prideful denial.

Of course, all the talent in the world won't flourish without the commensurate dose of drive, motivation, and ambition to succeed. This is really a given. What we are distinguishing between is not the talented good worker and the talented poor worker. We are discussing what makes one good worker more suitable for a job than another good worker.

The more talented the individual, the less their pay will matter to them than professional respect, room to exercise talent, and an inner feeling of contributing to the organization. These are the things that matter *most* to the most talented individuals. As a result, they better be the things the management pays attention to!

WHY IT MATTERS

Management is indeed about people, and connecting to their passions and talents in the orchestration of achieving business objectives. This should not be overlooked just because it can be. The cost is simply too high. Even though they may be hidden costs, they are the ones that kill the bottom line even if the top line revenue is high. You are equipping people for lifelong service to your company and your brand. Customers for life; brand loyalty—these are the things companies are seeking in their customers. Why aren't they seeking them in their employees?

Current business magazines and the Internet are full of wonderful stories of companies committing to the process, and reaping the great benefits in margin and productivity. These stories should inspire leaders and managers to find what works for them, because a customized fit will be much more effective than blanketing the company with somebody else's ideas. Analyze what others are doing, then make it your own, special to your organization and your people.

POISON CONTROL

Find out how your rate on the toxic scale. Read the following statements, giving yourself a 1 if you rarely do what the statement says, and a 10 if you consistently do what the statement says. If you are brave enough, have your staff rate these statements for your department, then consider the results carefully.

Rate yourself on a scale of 1-10

_____ I can clearly articulate my company's brand and value offering. Everyone who works for me can also clearly articulate the same.
Brand Statement: _____
_____

_____ My department head has a weekly meeting with me to keep me updated on projects and plans, and I have a weekly meeting with my staff to do the same.

_____ My company has a clear process for sharing annual and quarterly goals with all employees, regardless of rank.

_____ I have a very clear understanding of how my work contributes to the overall company strategic plan. In my department, every employee also has a good understanding of how their work contributes to the overall company goals.

_____ My company has a training program in place for employees, and it is well publicized so that every employee knows what classes are held, when they are held, and whether they are eligible to attend.

_____ I can list at least three reasons why talented employees would rather work at my company than the competitor's.

•

•

•

_____ I would recommend employment at my company to my family and good friends.

_____ My company encourages career development and succession planning for all employees, regardless of rank or pay scale.

_____ I regularly review my staff's qualifications and job performance to evaluate whether anyone is ready for career advancement.

_____ My company encourages employees to help solve problems by regularly asking for input and implementing their ideas.

Total your score: _____
The higher the score, the healthier your pond; the lower the score, the more toxic your pond. Make it your goal in the coming months to increase your score on each statement.

Clean Up Method 2: Celebrate and Give Credit

You have it easily in your power to increase the sum total of this world's happiness now. How? By giving a few words of sincere appreciation to someone who is lonely or discouraged.

Perhaps you will forget tomorrow the kind words you say today, but the recipient may cherish them over a lifetime.

--Dale Carnegie

Why is every great victory and achievement followed by spontaneous celebration? From the winning score in the big game to the ribbon cutting at a new building site, from a successful rocket launch to a baby's first steps, victory and achievement produce celebration deep in the heart of humanity. The practice of praising individuals for their accomplishments spans generations, cultures, nations, and all differences between people. *Praise* is defined as the act of *expressing warm approval or admiration of, to speak positively about.* It's simple: everybody celebrates.

What's true for all of humanity *outside* the workplace is also true for humanity *inside* the workplace: praise is a basic part of the human response system. So why is it often so completely absent?

Because *Deadly Toxins 2 & 3: The Blame Game* and *Ignoring Burnout* poison the pond and kill the celebratory moments that would appear spontaneously in any other context. These Toxins spread a feeling of uselessness and a sense of exhaustion that prevent a basic part of humanity from functioning properly.

The Toxin of the Blame Game sets up impossible situations with impossible expectations, then punishes the mistake-makers as if they were wayward children, not grown adults in an agreement with employers to perform work for a certain wage and benefit. This Toxin kills initiative and drive, destroys creative problem solving, hinders effective work, and also reduces profitability. The Blame Game also produces a sense of powerlessness, which leads to the feeling that no contribution will make a difference in the environment.

The Toxin of Ignoring Burnout overloads employees with work and requires their continual availability to the office, roping them in with 24/7 access through laptops and Blackberries. Individuals begin to question whether or not they truly possess the skills they thought they did, and become mired in powerlessness and apathy.

These Toxins can be reduced and eliminated by leaders and managers who **Celebrate and Give Credit** to their employees. This clean up method involves understanding the two basic needs of all of humanity and how to meet them in the workplace. Celebrating and Giving Credit means creating a workplace environment in which people can do the same thing they do in the rest of their lives: be happy and receive praise when they do something good. It's really that simple.

THE TWO BASIC NEEDS OF ALL HUMANITY

As discussed in Part I, the evolution of management theory has mirrored the evolution of business. Moving from a predominately agricultural and/or factory production economy to a service-based or "idea" economy has produced a correspondingly huge amount of thought on how and why people do what they do in the workplace. The theories have explored every aspect of human behavior and motivation, and have produced many viable and thought-provoking ideas, though no one has yet produced a theory that is universally considered "complete." Many of the terms are familiar: nature vs. nurture, Maslow's Hierarchy of Needs, social context, autonomy and relatedness, and so forth. Each theory slices the motivational pie into thinner wedges; however, in the end all of the theories boil down to this: humanity has two basic needs. They are the need to feel valued, and the need to contribute to something meaningful. All other human needs, and there are many, can be placed into one of these categories.

These two needs are deep-seated and divine; they are rooted in our souls. Some feel the needs more strongly than others, but they are present in all of us. Whatever the processes of childhood, upbringing, training, and genetics that form the personality and drive of individuals, they all still seek to have these two basic needs met somewhere.

Sometimes, sadly, individuals get twisted by dysfunction, and do not learn or self-reflect enough to shed their deviations from the norms of social behavior. For example, the only manner in which a person may feel valued is in the devaluation of others. These types of distortions cannot be left at home. When the leader or manager or employee leaves the house to go to work, they take themselves with them. The dysfunctional manager gets to work and practices dysfunctional management. This is how the toxins spread to begin with. Nevertheless, throughout the sum of our day, week, month, and lifetime, the need to feel valued and to contribute to something meaningful persists, and drives us.

Being celebrated and honestly praised and thanked for a job well done feeds the need to be valued far more than a paycheck. Money is always an important factor in any job situation, both for the employee and the employer. The employee must satisfy their basic economic needs through the paycheck. The employer must find employees to do the work at the price they are willing to pay. However, if you consistently pay average or lower than average salaries and wages, you can never expect to get better than average performance.

The opposite, however, is not true—a large paycheck will not necessarily guarantee you a talented workforce, because hiring talent and retaining talent are two completely different things. You may initially attract talent with a large sum of money; you will not keep talent with money alone. Talented employees often feel the two basic needs even more strongly than the rest, so when the opportunity to have them met is absent, and the pond is dysfunctional and toxic, they will not likely stay to fight on. Most individuals do have choices about where they seek work; the most talented employees have the most choices. To keep them in your pond, you may have to clean it up.

CELEBRATION EMPOWERS

What truly motivates individuals in the workplace? Achieving success, and being appreciated for the effort. Success and appreciation of success are of course predicated upon the practice of matching the employee with tasks or responsibilities they can master. If an employee cannot be generally and daily successful in the job, this point of empowerment is never reached. But even if daily success in the job is a given, the absence of praise and recognition is poison to the pond.

The Clean Up Method of Celebration and Giving Credit establishes empowerment, creates excitement about contribution, and drives the employee forward. Humans need this additional stimulus from the environment to truly thrive, because they are not on autopilot; there is a give and take at work as there is in every relationship and environment. When the environment is poisonous, the employees get poisoned, and it affects the work. What the environment is stimulating, challenging and celebratory, the employees have potential to reach astonishing results.

Unfortunately the Clean Up Method of Celebrate and Give Credit consists of the very thing that is hard for a toxic manager to express: sincere appreciation for the work of others. The same ego and insecurity that drives the Blame Game and Ignoring Burn Out blunts the recognition and sincere appreciation of another's efforts. As noted in Part I, this *is the environment that...employees suffer through when their leaders are not emotionally equipped to be in charge, and give into the need to make someone around them uncomfortable.*

It is remarkable how much simple encouragement can fuel the human spirit to keep on giving and giving. In an environment of celebration, where one's achievements and accomplishments are acknowledged, employees feel as though they can conquer the world. The external climate of celebration translates into internal motivation for the individual. Even better, when celebration is coupled with empowerment to get the job done, employees feel they can tackle real workplace problems and contribute to real solutions. Honestly, there is no stopping a talented employee with access to resources and the internal motivation to move the business forward.

When the managers and the employees are aware of their specific role in the overall plan of the company's objectives, there is always much to celebrate. Targets can be identified and hit, then celebrated. Milestones can be identified and

129

passed, then celebrated. But when nobody really knows what the end goal is for the day, week, month, quarter, year....how can much of anything be celebrated? Without knowing how their individual roles fit into the big picture, employees can lose motivation like a slow leaking tire, until they are flat and no longer functioning. The Clean Up Method of Celebrating and Giving Credit destroys the sense of powerlessness that can creep in, because individuals know where they fit, and what specific problems they are solving.

The human spirit needs hope for fuel. Hope is what keeps us alive in the darkest moments—hope that things will get better and turn around; hope that things will one day be different. Things are no different in the workplace. When the employees gather in the break room and say things like, "I just hope it gets better." "I hope it will be different after the New Year." "I hope that manager can make a difference around here." They are speaking to their level of being poisoned in a toxic workplace. Without this hope, getting out of bed to come to the workplace becomes increasingly difficult.

APPRECIATION FOR ALL

It would truly be a sweet world if all leaders and managers were concerned about establishing a beneficial workplace for employees, but that is a rather Pollyanna view of reality. Fortunately there is a stronger motivator for those who don't care much about the human cost. Companies simply won't get the best performance from their people unless they pay attention to these Toxins and provide the Clean Up Methods. Without best performance, the company cannot and will not reach its highest potential and best profitability. This indeed should be important to every leader and manager.

Fear doesn't motivate for best performance, but appreciation does. Fear limits creativity and creative problem solving; appreciation makes it blossom. The mind is let loose to think creatively and not be bound by "getting in trouble." The work environment shouldn't feel like the principal's office, or like waiting for Dad to come home and mete out your punishment. Nobody should be scared to go to work! Instead, the work environment should be a place of celebration, where appreciation is handed out in abundance. The work environment should be a place where employees are passionate about what specific goal they will achieve that day, knowing that the team and their boss and the entire company will benefit from their presence on the job, and in the annual goals and achievement of the entire company.

As a nation and as a culture, we are sorely lacking in appreciation. Sarcasm, cynicism and doubt have become the norm from grade school on up. A heart-felt thank you is hard to get from anybody these days, which makes it even more important at the workplace.

Appreciation is simply the recognition and enjoyment of the good qualities of someone or something. To appreciate means to recognize the full worth of something. It's popular to say that a company is only as good as its people; but are your employees truly something you consider valuable? The word *appraise* is from the same root as *appreciate*; it means that you evaluate something as worth prizing, worthy of praise. How do you measure up to this standard in your own workplace with your own staff?

Some leaders feel if they appreciate their employees' efforts at regular intervals, the employees will stop working so hard to achieve it. "I will save my praise for when something really dramatic happens!" is the cry of an emotionally stunted manager. This dysfunctional manager is applying her own brokenness to the rest of the world. Human nature simply doesn't work that way. Encouragement and appreciation inspire and motivate. Withholding it doesn't get the employee to work harder to get it; instead it fosters discouragement and burn out.

It's actually quite easy to show appreciation. Giving a round of applause is free. So clap in a meeting when attention is put on someone who did a good job. Leaders and managers should treat people like they matter, because they do. Make a conscious effort to praise and celebrate your team's successes. Keep an eye open for opportunities to praise. You will begin to see them everywhere.

EVERYDAY HEROES

Opportunities abound all day every day to Celebrate and Give Credit at the workplace. Every meeting is a perfect forum for recognizing and appreciating everyday heroes. Rounds of applause, thank you's, high fives, and well done's passed round will sustain the individuals and get them excited about attending far more than coffee and donuts. Recognizing staff, however, begs the question as to whether the manager knows and understands *what* to recognize. If there is no understanding the company's overall goals and vision, or where the team fits into it, how can milestones be celebrated?

Look around and be observant of your team. Who prevented a stock-out by noticing a forgotten inventory level? Who managed a product launch or completed a shift error free? Who has the highest safety rating? Who completed the week with no errors in the cash drawer? Get the other leaders and managers talking about their staff and incidents worthy of praise. Every department can find a daily task to celebrate, even if it is small in terms of the company's (or department's) overall goals. Those daily tasks are still important to the individuals functioning in that department.

Simple moments of celebration and credit can make a huge impact on an employee's day. One CEO would carry a sheet of expressive (and inexpensive!) stickers with her during the day. When the opportunity came up to congratulate someone on a job well done, or if an individual had a good suggestion at a meeting, or anything worthy of celebration, she would hand them a sticker. The employees would proudly wear the stickers all day long, and then keep them on their cube walls. Obviously it's not the sticker they cherished, but the appreciation.

Celebrating and Giving Credit does not have to cost anything. But the company who truly wants to establish a culture of appreciation will reserve resources for the annual company picnic, or annual awards and bonuses and gifts to employees, or the occasional movie tickets or ball game seats.

Most companies have some form of the annual picnic—a time where employees and their families eat hot dogs or bar-b-que, and the company says *thank you* for all your efforts. The annual picnic can be a fine expression of gratitude, but don't let it stop with a hot dog and 10-minute thank you speech from the already-bored CEO who would rather be back at the office answering emails and making calls. At Graniterock, the executive team takes the annual picnic to a new level. They call it "Recognition Day," and each department and facility takes turns bragging about its accomplishments. The whole company celebrates the efforts of each department, and the human need of feeling valued and appreciated is met in these individuals.

The company keeps a "Recognition Day Book" chock full of the multitude of moments during the year when employees were recognized and celebrated. From attending training classes to winning company awards, to features on Employee of the Month, to recognition for cash bonuses paid out to hundreds of staff members as incentives and thank you's, the book is an obvious and weighty statement about the company's commitment to Celebrating and Giving Credit. No, a Recognition Book is not a cure-all for company woes, but it is indeed a place to start battling Toxins.

THE GENERATION GAP STRIKES AGAIN

For Generation Xers (born between 1965 and 1979) and Millennium's (those born after 1979 but who's end date is not yet identified) fun is not something to be had *outside* work. In the mid-1980's when giant corporations like IBM and EDS made the decision to allow male employees to wear colored shirts with their coats and ties, it was considered a celebratory event. Yes, it's true, white shirts and suits were thought to bring a work ethic with them into the office. Whether or not corporate culture has suffered from the influx of colored shirts and their aftermath of casual dress every day, it hardly matters now. Those employers who don't incorporate fun into their environment will simply lose out on the best young talent. These upcoming generations don't separate work from the rest of their lives the way their predecessors did, and do. And no matter how hard the old guard wishes it were so, or even insists it were so, it isn't and won't be. These generations are sometimes called the "entitlement generations," and one thing they firmly believe they are entitled to is a non-boring life at the workplace.

Generation X employees work hard and play hard, and like the experiences to mix. They prefer "the art of living" to gathering material goods, and would rather receive movie tickets or a weekend trip than a service plaque or 5-year pin. As parents, Generation Xers also place a very high value on family time and family life. The old "quality time" cry of Boomers who wanted to justify their ten minutes a night with the kids before bed makes no headway with these parents. They want quality time *and* quantity time!

The freedom of casual dress days just isn't enough to impress these workers. But flex time and more workplace choice will. Leaders and managers who wish to engage the best talent must pay attention to the changing demographics of the available workforce, or once again risk losing (or never gaining) the best talent in the pond.

BUILDING BONDS BEYOND WORK

Celebration is also about building bonds between employees and fostering teamwork. One manager in a software sales company required each of his employees to bring a picture of a tangible goal they were setting each quarter. They ran the company bonus structure on a quarter basis, but this was strictly his idea that he used with his group of six salespeople. He had put up a large bulletin board in their break area, and on the first Monday morning of the new quarter, each employee brought in a picture representing their goal for the quarter. The goals ranged from getting out of debt to buying new bikes for the kids, to vacation, to spa day, to jewelry, to new golf clubs to everything under the sun. The group spent the first Monday morning meeting of the quarter telling each other about their goal and why they chose it. The enthusiasm was contagious and effective—each cup of coffee in the break room reminded them all of what specific goal they were striving for this quarter.

Not only did they have their own goal manifested in a picture to keep them motivated, but they also encouraged one other in the pursuit. And they learned quite a bit about each other outside their roles at the office. Katy was recently divorced and wanted to get her toddler a new tricycle—when she had to use the bonus money instead on a doctor bill, another employee gave her one her son had just outgrown. When people appreciate and thank one another, and strive for goals together and celebrate achievements, they build bonds and their success matters to each of them. When struggles arise in the workplace, the bonds that have been built through these kinds of activities help sustain the team.

These individuals are not likely to leave for another pond out of frustration.

This principle will manifest itself in thousands of different ways across thousands of different companies. Celebration, bond-building, appreciation and fun do not need formulas; they need leaders and managers who *pay attention* and who genuinely care for the well-being of their workforce.

Once again, as in all things important, authenticity cannot be faked. There is a story of a corporate manager who attended a workshop on building more praise for staff into their routines. For some individuals this means to go on autopilot, and issue thanks you's and praises at marked intervals, rather than paying attention to true opportunities. One manager found it easiest to send an email at the end of the day to his staff, thanking them for the work that day and praising their efforts. He didn't actually engage with the employees to find something specific to thank them for, rather it was a blanket email; a response to something he learned in a workshop. As a result, the employees found the praise to be what it was—false. In one instance the manager sent a "praise" email to an employee who had called in sick and gone to the ball game. He read it the next morning when he arrived; the boss thanking him for the work he had done when he'd actually been eating a hot dog and drinking a beer in the sun. That doesn't count as true appreciation.

WHY IT MATTERS

People want to feel valued, and they want to contribute to something meaningful. These needs are rooted deep within humanity's molecular soul structure. With the Clean Up Method of Celebration and Giving Credit, these needs are met and the business moves forward, solving problems and increasing in productivity and profitability.

Additionally, happy employees are your very best brand statement. Word of mouth is still considered the most powerful form of advertising, and your employees advertise your brand in the community everywhere they go.

POISON CONTROL

Rate yourself on the following statements, giving yourself a 1 if you rarely do what the statement says, and a 10 if you consistently do what the statement says. If you are brave enough, have your staff rate these statements for your department, then consider the results carefully.

Rate yourself on a scale of 1-10

_____ My company has a recognition program for employees that awards employees for years of service, great accomplishments, above and beyond work, creative problem solving, and money-saving ideas.

_____ My department has implemented _____ ideas over the last six months that have come from staff members.

_____ I regularly solicit feedback and information from the staff executing the projects rather than only passing information down from above.

_____ I can name the top producers in my department and in my company.

_____ The last time we celebrated company successes was _____. The entire company did this: ____
_____.

_____ I have a recognition plan in place in my department that mirrors the company plan, but is centered around my team to build unity.

___ I have outlined specific milestones or achievement levels for my department that coincide with the company's overall vision and strategy.

_____ I take my team to lunch or bring in a treat once per
_____ to celebrate their work efforts and build unity.

___ It is not unusual to hear other teams in the building celebrating one success or another with applause, or seeing balloons tied to chairs, or to hear discussions among the staff of what special incentive they've enjoyed such as movie tickets, ball park tickets, dinner certificates, or other experience-related bonuses.

_____ It has been less than 30 days since my boss showed appreciation for my work through a tangible object such as a bonus, tickets, a card, or even an email of thanks. It has been less than 30 days since I have done the same for my staff.

___ It has been less than 30 days since my boss verbally expressed appreciation for my work with a Thank you, or other verbal expression. It has been less than 30 days since I have done the same for my staff..

Total your score: _____
The higher the score, the healthier your pond; the lower the score, the more toxic your pond. Make it your goal in the coming months to increase your score on each statement.

Clean Up Method 3: Build Community

*Without a sense of caring, there can be
no sense of community.*

--Anthony J. D'Angelo

The workplace has changed considerably over the last 50 years. To those entering the workforce in the 1960s, a solid job with a known corporation meant 40 years and a pension. But expectations of the workplace are simply a reflection of society's expectations, and they are in continual evolution. Leaders and managers that choose to ignore this do so at their peril—the best talent will follow the companies who meet the changing expectations. The younger the talent, the more hooked they are on freedom, flexibility and meaningful work. Empowerment and teamwork is the battle cry of the times, from HGTV's design series to Do It Yourself magazines to Lowe's hardware store's motto, "Let's Build Something Together."

The cultural shift from hiring experts to becoming experts ourselves and partnering with others to achieve our desires filters through all aspects of our lives and on into the workplace. Employees are no longer satisfied with simply being told what to do and doing it. Individuals are seeking a more satisfying day in the workplace along with everywhere else in their lives.

This drive manifests itself in an eagerness for teamwork, authority and decision-making capability, and empowerment.

But *Deadly Toxin 4: Measuring by Method* stifles and prevents this sort of progress at the workplace. In an environment of Measuring by Method, the *how* matters more than the *what*, and is spread by leaders and managers who feel the need to control their employees out of their own insecurity and fear. This Toxin kills the drive of the most talented employees and frustrates the ability to move the business forward by squashing contribution. Leaders and managers who practice Measuring by Method cannot let go of micromanaging their staff. Measuring by Method by its nature creates a lack of trust at the workplace, as employees are deprived of creative problem solving and of bringing answers to the table.

This Toxin can be reduced and eliminated by leaders and managers who **Build Community** at the workplace. Building Community starts with the foundation of a culture of Celebrating and Giving Credit (Clean Up Method 2). As the two basic needs of humanity are met with celebration and credit, building a community takes these principles to a deeper level. People want opportunities to make their time matter. The values and mission statement of the company are important, the charity the company practices is important, and the work itself is important. Building Community pays attention to these needs and desires, and satisfies them in the workplace.

This clean up examines human group behavior, and what motivates individuals to stay the course in times of difficulty as well as in times of bounty. Connecting emotionally with the people who drive the business forward and empowering them to do their jobs well is at the heart of Building Community.

THE HOME GOES TO WORK

Paying attention to what is important to talented employees, and in particular the *upcoming pool* of talented employees, will make a difference to any company's bottom line profitability. It's too important to ignore. The committed workers of yesteryear were those individuals who stayed at the office to work. The new generation of committed workers might work just as many hours, but they bring the *home* into the office with them. This may happen literally, with companies who encourage telecommuting for some employees who actually stay in their homes to work, or manifest itself at the office with companies that provide "home" services in the workplace such as laundry, oil changes, and even haircuts. When companies commit resources to caring for their workers in benefits, workplace comforts or conveniences, they are repaid ten-fold with loyalty and ROI.

The Container Store early on paid attention to building a community among its employees, rather than treating them as simply workers to be bossed around. The Container Store has brought the home to the workplace in several ways, including offering employees free yoga classes three times a week, providing on-site dry cleaning and car washes, and allowing employees the full use of the postal and packaging center. Take a lesson from The Container Store here— what area of *your business* can you offer as a service to your employees as well as your customers?

Most people *work* more hours in a day than they do any other activity. They spend more time with their co-workers than their family members, and they make sacrifices for the job they might not make for anyone else. It should be clear that the manner in which the time is spent is important. Work is a place the employee has to be eight hours a day— more and more individuals are demanding that it also be a place they want to be. There's a reason that nearly half of all workers feel disconnected from their employers—because in nearly half of the existing companies, employers do not successfully Build Community.

Sometimes company leaders fear that employees with costly or unusual perks will end up taking advantage of them, as if their investment in the effort will produce a lazy or ungrateful employee. They are quite simply misguided. Company leaders do not need to worry about employees taking advantage of their workplace perks.

Next Wave Logistics provides web-based sales tools for companies in the direct selling industry. With a recognizable client list including such names as The Pampered Chef, Creative Memories, and PartyLite among others, the company has gone from startup in 1999 to nearly $15 million in 2007, with an annual increase of about 150% per year.

Is it surprising that every one of Next Wave's 53 employees telecommute from their homes across the U.S. and from as far away as Spain? But Harold Zimmerman and Dave Proctor, the company's co-founders, aren't worried about anybody taking advantage. Says Zimmerman, "Our employees love the environment we've established and give us back thankfulness and hard work. We've never had a problem with anyone taking advantage of the situation because the loyalty is so strong."

Next Wave is building community in true global fashion. Senior Software Engineer Jesus Infantes has been with the company from its early days. He is incredibly talented, and had done amazing work for the company. He came to see Harold and Dave one day with a heavy heart, telling them that he and his wife wanted to move back to Spain, that his wife's family needed them, and it was time to go home. Jesus hated leaving Next Wave, and Harold couldn't bear to lose him, so he simply said, "You don't have to leave. We'll figure out a way for you to work from Spain." And they did. Next Wave kept his institutional knowledge, kept the inspiration that he is to the company, kept projects on track and revenue uninterrupted, and more than all of that, generated a loyalty and passion in a talented employee that will likely never extinguish.

CHANGING EXPECTATIONS

The generation of employees swelling the ranks today and their upcoming replacements value quality time with family and their own freedom. Employers will be forced to change to gain even nominal talent, since the number of "replacement" employees is smaller than the pool of current employees. There are only 56 million Generation Xers and Millennium's to replace the 76 million retiring Baby Boomers. These generations value "relationships" and "experiences," which do not include being tied to a laptop on a family vacation, or even missing baseball practice on a weeknight.

What employers need to understand is that if they can bring themselves to Build Community and practice the other Clean Up Methods in this book, the changes they have to make to the workplace won't be sacrifices. Well, there may be one sacrifice: hiring more employees in HR to manage the flood of resumes and work requests that will pour in. As mentioned previously, Patagonia receives 900 resumes for every one job opening. Google receives 1300 resumes every day. Do you think they have any trouble at all hiring the absolute best talent for the available position?

Many leaders and managers will feel the greatest obstacle to Building Community is that it does indeed cost money. Sometimes lots of money. The cost of a good health care plan, especially for small employers, can be very daunting. Onsite child care is expensive. Gym facilities, paid time off, good food in the employee cafeteria—everything costs something. But doing nothing costs a great deal more. The bottom line return in terms of employee retention alone can justify a large cost investment in the human component. The enormity of lost opportunity, lost institutional knowledge, lost history of mistakes, lost time in rebuilding teamwork are just the tip of the iceberg of losses when you've hired a great employee and then lose them due to the toxins in your pond. You also risk gaining a reputation in the marketplace that makes it hard to get and retain the best talent. Now that can get expensive.

When Patagonia was begun in the 1970's, the owners and their friends who worked with them had small children, and they brought them to work. In this sense, on-site child care has been a part of the company from the very beginning. But as the company grew, it became impossible to keep cribs next to desks, so resources were committed to developing a special area for the children.

Today, their operation includes on-site day care facilities that charge a tuition rate, subsidies for employees who need them, and company buses to take and pick up children from school. But they didn't stop there. Caring for the physical needs of children is only one aspect of Building Community. Patagonia reaches out to the values of its employees by allowing five days off in its benefit package for parents to participate in their children's activities *during* the workday. These parents don't miss school plays, holiday parties in the classroom, or any other activity for their children because they can't get off work. Don't you think a parent who isn't stressing out over missing a child's important event will contribute a higher level of effort at the workplace? If your answer is "no", then you simply don't understand human nature, and the loyalty that Building Community creates in an employee base. Yes, it all costs money. But an internal cost analysis at Patagonia compared the cost of the day care operation to the cost of turnover and lost work and found that it was more expensive to lose the talented employees, especially the women. It costs money to care. It costs more money not to.

At Next Wave, the business is software development, implementation and hosting. The hours can get a little crazy sometimes, but when the call comes in for all hands on deck, Next Wavers are up to the task. "Everyone knows," says Zimmerman, "that if they work in the evening after the kids go to bed, they are then free to take a long morning. We can't run our business in confined business hours, but we give back the time in very flexible ways."

Google has become well known for its crazy generous perks, such as *free* gourmet meals at nearly a dozen different cafeterias and cafes at the headquarters. But on a more practical basis, Google management Builds Community by connecting on a very basic level with employees. Understanding that working long hours puts stress on individuals to manage the rest of life's tasks, Google provides onsite haircuts, oil changes, dry cleaning and car washes. They will even reimburse employees for up to $500 in take out food over the first four weeks of a new baby's arrival in the household. That is a very creative way to show appreciation and connect with employees.

One of the advantages of cleaning toxins out of the pond is that misdeeds and bad conduct tend to surface by themselves. The positive peer pressure of the other employees who won't allow one attitude to ruin it for the rest of them will self-police. Will a new mother, required to return to work by her financial standing and frantic to find suitable day care work less hard if her employer provides an onsite day care? Of course not! She has peace of mind, she gains time not having to drop the baby off somewhere far away, and most importantly, she is freed from what could be the greatest worry of her day—her child's well-being. Her company has connected with her deepest humanity. And, she will help keep the program going by policing offenders.

Funding a day care may not be in your capital budget for next year, but you can surely do *something* to Build Community at your workplace. What will it be?

THAT PESKY EMOTIONAL CONNECTION

No doubt there are many toxic companies who can nail the textbook definition of sound management principles— they have read all the books, completed all the workbooks, even had brown bag lunches and requisite quarterly planning meetings with the whiteboard and the giant stickie pads covering the walls. But they return to their workaday world, teeming with the Seven Deadly Toxins, and never connect the dots that the appearance of soundness is not the same thing as soundness. They never make the emotional connection necessary to Build Community in their workplace. It's critical to understand that adopting an HR program, or bringing in a motivational speaker for a two-day workshop isn't the same thing as building a healthy and robust workplace. This is not a one-shot deal, or a series of one-shots. It is a dedicated, consistent and authentic commitment to change, and to caring, focused on the humanity of your workforce.

How do you tell the difference between a pretend Build Community company and a real Build Community company? By checking the health of the pond inhabitants. Turnover is a very solid indicator of workplace health and emotional connectivity, or the lack of it. If your turnover is not significantly lower than the industry average, and you cannot account for the reasons, then your pond is simply not as healthy as it could be. People don't leave work they enjoy in a healthy environment and people they are connected to.

As noted in Part I,
employees are individual bundles of energy, motivation, compassion, and desire for achievement. They are a mix of every experience of their upbringing and education, of their interactions and gene pool.... As they continue to contribute and continue to be rewarded and recognized, they hope to be promoted or challenged at another level, to continue improve-

*ment and moving forward. They want to be sup-
ported by their bosses, believed in by management,
and respected by their peers.*

Understanding this to be the make up of employees means
you have a better chance at motivating them to deliver their
highest and best performance at the workplace, no matter
what their job description. Isn't part of your goal as a leader
or manager to elevate your company higher than the competition? Being better than the competition in part means
you must be willing to do what they are not willing to do. In
many cases, the competition is unwilling to invest in the emotional well-being of its employees by Building Community
and focusing on those things important to their workforce.
In some tightly competitive industries, your workplace environment may be your only advantage.

Most companies view their employees as an expense.
Salaries, benefits, paid vacation, personal days, bonuses and
other costs all add up for the company making the decision to
hire an individual. But another aspect of the changing times
is that employees are now considering employment at a company in their terms of cost and benefit. They ask, "What is
it going to cost *me* to go to work for *you*?" If the cost to their
values is too high, they will move on to another pond.

Employees want their judgment to be trusted. The
reciprocal action on the company's part is to make sure the
employee is *trust-worthy*. This book does not advocate keeping untalented or destructive employees in the workplace.
Keeping an individual who should be let go only helps *all* of
the toxins spread. Keeping an employee who should be let
go does not show kindness to the employee or to the other
employees on the team. In fact, it is very disrespectful to
all the truly hard-working employees, as the load is often
distributed among them, and they suffer the burden. Additionally you run the risk of driving away your talent, as they

lose respect for your judgment as a leader. At Next Wave, Zimmerman says they've gotten pretty good at determining during the interview process who will work out and who won't. "When we hire someone who then doesn't fit, we take steps to improve their performance, but we have an ethical responsibility to our clients and other employees not to keep unproductive people," he says. "It's not fair for anyone, so we let them go pretty fast."

COMMON GOALS AND VISION

According to Jim Collins, co-author of "Built to Last: Successful Habits of Visionary Companies" (HarperCollins Publishers Inc., 1994), companies with strong missions consistently produce higher results than those companies solely focused on the bottom line. And no wonder—these are the companies that are Building Community among their employees and meeting the basic needs of humanity in the process.

But don't be fooled; writing the mission statement is the easy part. Living up to it, embodying it, bringing it to life, making it more than a tag line is the hard part.

Mission based companies must make sure their mission is for their employees as well as their customers. Too many companies are so focused on the customer, whom they treat as kings, that they neglect the staff and really treat them more like indentured servants to the king. What they don't realize is that the two must go hand-in-hand. Employees are customers, even more, they are your brand advertisers, and you send them out into the world every day to support or oppose your brand, depending upon how you treat them at the workplace. A company that sacrifices it employees to serve its customers will never produce to its fullest potential.

Common goals and vision give people something to hang onto. Humanity is about grouping--we are always looking for common purposes and common bonds with others. It's true in life; it's true at work. Ask yourself, what does my company stand for? What is my company committed to? What do I stand for? What am I committed to? What can I do in my area to instill passion and commitment in my workforce? Answering these questions and acting on the answers will change the dynamics in your workplace.

At Patagonia, it's company policy to take a break if the local surf conditions are good. Located in Ventura Beach, CA, it's not unusual for the building to empty out mid-morning if conditions look fine. The company is staffed by avid outdoor-lovers, and this company policy builds community on several different levels. First, it feeds the employee's passions and provides them with opportunities to do what they love. But even deeper than that, the company policy is a statement of trust from the management: get your work done, and don't miss any opportunity to enjoy the surf. Founder Yvon Chouinard doesn't worry about employees taking advantage and that is true payoff for building a community. He makes sure he hires the right people, then he gives them freedom, autonomy and respect. Enough freedom, autonomy and respect to trust them to do their jobs *and* enjoy the company's philosophy. The lesson here is that Building Community is possible—you *can* do something.

When a company supports charitable causes, it gives the employees a great place to rally. Participating as a company on a Habitat for Humanity build, collecting money together at intersections for the Labor Day Muscular Dystrophy Marathon, sponsoring a blood drive, or any other group activity that supports a worthy cause builds community within the workplace. When employees have reason to spend quality time together outside the workplace working together for the good of something bigger than themselves, it fosters a deeper appreciation between them and a greater bond to the company that makes it possible.

Celeste Ford, CEO of Stellar Solutions, an aerospace consulting firm, has found a way to build community at her company by engaging the value system of her employees. Through the Stellar Solutions Foundation, the company allocates money per each employee to be donated to the charity of their choice. Ford believes this approach empowers her employees to get involved in the community, and feel supported by their employer in causes that matter to them. The recipients of the donations have included a wide variety of charities such as community-based groups to serve the needy, preservation societies, and medical research organizations.

But even charitable giving can be twisted to a toxic agenda. In some large corporations, enormous peer pressure exists to contribute to the company's chosen charity over and over. When lower salaried and hourly workers are called into a manager's office by someone two and three levels above them to be "talked into" contributing to the program, the authenticity of the community is truly in question. Forced participation will never get the same results as authentic rallying around a cause.

THE VALUE OF AN EDUCATION

The term "Renaissance Man" once described an individual who had mastered the world's body of knowledge in languages, philosophies, theologies, mathematics, and the sciences. That was in a time when the world's body of knowledge could be known and articulated, and an entire field of study may not change much in any one lifetime. Thomas Jefferson and Benjamin Franklin are widely considered the last of the true Renaissance Men. It is now estimated from various sources that the world's body of knowledge doubles somewhere between every 14 months to every five years. It's been over 150 years since any one individual could come close to learning and articulating the world's body of knowledge in the arts and sciences. In fact, even the term "Renaissance Man" has dropped from common speech and is considered "anachronistic," or seriously old-fashioned.

Today it is difficult to be master of all knowledge in a specific field, much less a variety of fields. Technological advances and the changes they bring to the workplace cause enormous differences within a two to three-year span. It is very unlikely that anyone's job will stay the same over their entire career anymore. Now more than ever ongoing training, retraining and skill development is essential, not just to the employee who needs a job, but also to the employers who want to keep their good workers.

Building a community of training and opportunity for employees encourages longevity, loyalty, and fights the very high cost of turnover. Why not train your existing employees and build their future *with* them? That way, your company becomes the beneficiary of their knowledge, wisdom and expertise, in addition to their loyalty. An enormous amount of time is lost bringing a new employee up to speed. This cost alone can compensate for the investment in training an existing employee to move forward. Plus, you gain institutional knowledge, loyalty, and all of those other things that can't truly be measured. Rehiring, retraining, rebuilding relationships, everyone learning everyone else's role, along with company history of what's worked and what hasn't.... it's all a colossal waste of time, energy and resources.

Employees who have been in their jobs for a long time also benefit from training and opportunities even if they are happy in their current work. Increased interest, engagement and new challenges will keep them fresh and engaged. Opportunity is the operative word here—this meets the basic needs of people to contribute to something meaningful.

If the management staff's view of training is "Why should I train my employees when they will just leave and go somewhere else?" then the manager doesn't at all understand what motivates people, and there are likely many toxins spreading around in that pond.

WHY IT MATTERS

One hundred years ago when communities were smaller, businesses lived or died by word of mouth advertising. What other individuals said about you or your company could send customers your way, or cause them to avoid your business. As the world expanded and communities became so large that one voice couldn't have such an affect, the importance of word of mouth advertising decreased. Businesses turned their attention to other forms of advertising. But the world has become a very small place once again with the Internet and all the informational access we all share. Thus, word of mouth is once again important.

Building Community at work makes building customer community easier, lending itself to achieving customer life-time value. Building Community is its own loyalty program.

POISON CONTROL

Rate yourself on the following statements, giving yourself a 1 if you rarely do what the statement says, and a 10 if you consistently do what the statement says. If you are brave enough, have your staff rate these statements for your department, then consider the results carefully.

Rate yourself on a scale of 1-10

____ My company builds community at our workplace by meeting the two basic needs of all humanity in tangible ways. I feel that I am valued at my job, and that I am contributing to something meaningful.

____ I created opportunities in my department for building community by doing the following:

•

•

•

____ My company supports charities and our local community. All the employees are encouraged to participate and contribute to something larger than ourselves and the products we sell.

____ The turnover rate at my company and in my department is significantly lower than the industry standard.

____ My company does not keep unproductive or destructive employees on the payroll for long.

____ At my company, principles drive business decisions.

_____ My company has an ongoing training and professional development program available to all staff members regardless of their rank.

_____ My department has a budget for team building activities.

_____ My boss trusts me to get my work done, and allows me the flexibility I need to attend to important events in my personal life.

_____ I trust my employees to get their work done, and allow them any flexibility they need as long as their job performance standards are met.

Total your score: _____
The higher the score, the healthier your pond; the lower the score, the more toxic your pond. Make it your goal in the coming months to increase your score on each statement.

Clean Up Method 4: Exercise Creative Discipline

*Discipline is the bridge between goals
and accomplishment.*

--Jim Rohn

Endless creativity exists all around us. The abundance of inspired beauty in nature, the remarkable expressions in art, and the limitless talent working in every industry today can generate more good ideas than could ever be put into play. Ahhh, that's the challenge. How does anyone say "no" to a beautiful, inspired, great idea? Should anyone ever say "no" to that? How do you decide what constraints to put in place, and what good ideas to develop and implement? When a creative individual is running a company or a department, and possesses a seemingly inexhaustible supply of ideas for programs, promotions, products, the risk comes not in having the well run dry, but in drowning everyone in the ensuing flood.

It's fabulous to have great ideas. But unless the idea can be translated into a value proposition for the business, it's merely a good idea. Not all good ideas need to be acted upon. But in an environment with *Deadly Toxins 5 & 6: Constant Fast and Revisiting Decisions* at work poisoning the pond, leaders and managers feel the need to implement every good idea that they have.

The Toxin of Constant Fast spreads its poison through the pond by requiring employees to work at a constantly fast pace, with no time for rebuilding resilience or margin. This Toxin wrecks employee morale, increases errors, costs more money and reduces profitability, all because humans aren't wired for the brutal pace of Constant Fast. Constant Fast eats away profits by destroying the margin, no matter what the top line generates in revenue. The manager to whom Constant Fast is normal pace may not even know what he is requiring from his staff. He would do well to pay attention to the health of the pond inhabitants, or risk losing his talented employees to more robust environments.

The Toxin of Revisiting Decisions creates a reactive mode of leadership in the workplace. Authority and responsibility are not balanced for the employees attempting to do good work. As others interfere with their jobs, they lose the authority to make decisions but are yet held accountable for results. This Toxin increases errors, destroys vendor relationships, costs money, and kills employee morale.

These Toxins can be reduced and eliminated by leaders and managers who **Exercise Creative Discipline** in the workplace. Creative Discipline employs time as a resource: time to think, time to perform, time to review. This clean up method involves slowing down long enough to create a thoughtful strategic plan, and committing appropriate resources to its execution. Creative Discipline means that the leadership is confident enough in their plan, and in the talent they've amassed to execute that plan, that they can draw a "stop line" in the sand and manage the process of good ideas. Exercising Creative Discipline gains you margin through productivity, reduced turnover, and applied passion and loyalty from happy employees.

DRUCKER ONCE AGAIN HITS THE MARK

Peter Drucker's most lasting legacy work may be his ideas on Management by Objectives (MBO), which he began to develop in the 1950's and are expounded in his 1954 book, *The Practice of Management.* Even in rapidly changing environments, these principles still set the groundwork for any good strategic plan created by any forward thinking organization today. The theory basically states that any organization should determine what its objectives are, then create a strategy to achieve them, and next build a tactical plan that executes the strategy. Drucker believed this practice should be levied throughout the entire organization, from top to bottom, no matter what the function of the department.

Essentially, the principles advocate formalizing the "good intentions" of leaders and managers by writing out what it is the work is attempting to achieve, and setting it to a specific timeline with measurable touchstones. Of course, setting the plan is only the first step. The plan must actually be put into action, and then tweaked and altered as obstacles arise. And of course, the plan must be embraced and encouraged from the top leadership or it will just dwindle into nothingness. No process will go to work on its own; human nature must be prodded along to keep going in the right direction. This is the essential nature of true Leadership: the ability to move the group forward and stay focused on the tasks necessary to reach the objective.

Over time, management theorists felt the need to add a strong leadership component to the process, which resulted in the Project Management approach. This approach tasks a specific individual (the project manager) with finding and allocating the appropriate resources, and keeping up with the completion percentages of the tasks. Providing this information to the team keeps the team moving in the appropriate direction. However, it's critical to realize that the ability

159

to discern obstacles and challenges, and recognize which of them truly require changes to the plan is a skill set and talent level present in an individual, not in the process itself. No process, however brilliant or seemingly all-encompassing, can substitute for talent. Drucker himself, in the 1990's commented on his own system, "It's just another *tool*. It is not the great cure for management inefficiency."

Both Toxins of Constant Fast and Revisiting Decisions will always prevent any process from working effectively because they distract the participants from the overall goals and objectives, and require them to focus on short-term fires or crises. After a series of short-term crises, it's easy to forget what the long-term stable goal even was.

Some current management theorists have dismissed Management by Objective as old-school, and inappropriate given today's need for flexible workplaces and structures. On the contrary, Drucker's "tool," as he described it, is a framework that can be adapted to any structure and to any sort of formality or lack thereof. At Next Wave, the reporting structure is basically flat—or as flat as the co-founders can get it. Harold and Dave are the organizational heads, and when there is an impasse, or if a unilateral decision needs to be made, they make it. But the "leader core" of the organization is comprised of about 9-10 individuals who interact with the rest of the 53-person staff with close accountabilities and constant communication. Remember that every one of the employees telecommutes from their homes, and it's clear that Next Wave has a very unorthodox structure. But for Harold and Dave, knowing where they are going and how they are going to get there is the key to their success.

Harold understands that the people he hires are more important than the structure he uses to define his organization. It's the *people* who will meet the objectives of the business, regardless of the structure. "I was continually amazed by companies that would ask the *what* before the *who*," Harold says. "They would need to fill a spot, and lay out the hierarchy and pick people to fill the spots. But truly," he emphasizes, "the people you pick will change the way you look at how you organize those spots. You can't confine talent like that."

BEGIN AT THE BEGINNING

Continually discussed in college classrooms, corporate boardrooms, in books and in lectures, all management theories attempt to define a process that will move the business forward. Whatever component or idea the theory focuses upon, the desirable outcome is to increase business and decrease obstacles. To that end, there are a few foundational blocks that many theories and practices share.

Persona. Who are you? Defining yourself and your company from the beginning prevents you from being reactively shoved into a corner and allowing the market or your competition to define you. What is your brand personality? Who is your target demographic? Where else does your customer shop? Buy groceries? Where do they live and what are they interested in? What are their hobbies? How does your product or service meet their needs? What are ten adjectives that describe your brand? These are all questions that form the persona of your company. If you cannot answer these questions right now in your mind as you read through them, then you and your team need to take some time to get the number one foundational block defined. If you work in an existing company and these things are not clearly defined, study your customer and then create the persona yourself. All of the answers are there; it's just a matter of focusing on them and pulling them together.

Vision or Mission Statements. Your persona can be worked into your overall company statement about who you are and what you do. But don't attempt to write your vision or mission statement without defining your persona first. If you work in an existing company and these things don't exist, formulate them. If no one else in leadership is interested in defining these things, then take on the responsibility to do it for your department. Get all of your employees together, define your department's persona within the scope of the company's product or service and customer demographic, and write a vision or mission statement for your department.

Company Goals. What defines success for your organization in 12 months, three years, and five years? What is your revenue target? Employee head count? Products and services offered? How many customers will you have? You must have a target in order to create a plan, because firing into the forest and then claiming whatever you hit as the target doesn't count as strategy. Company Goals is also where you can specify the initiatives you plan over the long term. Building expansion, voice over IP, new product lines, new market expansion—all of these count as initiatives that should be strategically planned, not stumbled into.

Objectives. Simply put, objectives are formal statements of what you want to achieve. The statements should have a few common characteristics, such as clear wording as to what's expected, clear understanding of who exactly is expected to do what, and when all of the tasks necessary to meet the objective should be completed. Often this process is obscured by someone's need to turn it into a huge spreadsheet with hundred of columns and checkpoints, interlinking and interlocking objectives and contingencies and emergencies and fire drills. Suddenly managing the project spreadsheet has become a greater task that doing the work! Keep it simple. What do you want to achieve? By when? How will you do it? How will you know if it's successful? These are the important questions.

Tactical Plan. This plan is made of the nitty-gritty, every day operational tasks that must be performed to meet the defined objectives. This is where the staff gets assigned specific daily roles. If the senior level manager is down at this level, engaged in the tactical details of the plan, you've got some toxins to clean up. Hire a talented and capable staff, and then let them tackle the business problems.

STACK RANK THE PRIORITIES

It's very easy to lose sight of what's to be done when reading through most managerial language. Formulation of strategies, collaborative strategies, opportunistic strategies, internal consistency, user's perspective, links and substrategies—huh, what?? Here it is, simply put: Decide the tasks you need to do in order to reach your objectives, then decide which one to do first.

A true priority list is stack-ranked, vertical, with only one priority occupying the top slot. Deciding what should be done first necessarily means that something else can't be done first. A priority list with more than one item listed as the top priority is just a list, not a *priority* list.

1. Most critical priority—(the item with the biggest business impact).
2. Next Priority
3. Next Priority
4. Next Priority
5. etc.

The criteria for ranking will be as unique as your company. Again, true leadership is necessary here to determine the appropriate criterion for creating and maintaining the priorities. Choosing a priority due to personal preference or someone's pet project are not really good ways to decide. The criterion will likely include your business environment, corporate objectives, new opportunities, opening markets, revenue gaps, industry drivers, and existing marketing strategies. The Toxins of Constant Fast and Revisiting Decisions simply cannot exist in a stack-ranked, thoughtful priority list formulated by a talented leader. They are mutually exclusive.

A good rule of thumb for development and implementation of the list would be to tackle the top three priorities with 80 percent of your resources, both budget and personnel. The next three priorities follow with the remaining 20 percent of your resources. As the top priorities are achieved and checked off, the list rotates up, bringing into immediate focus what had been on the back burner. Working in this manner also allows you the time needed to evaluate the remaining list to determine whether the items still warrant funding, long before it has been allocated. For example, you might find the No. 4 slot on your list is inadvertently satisfied in conjunction with another priority, or that No. 2 is no longer valid.

This isn't to say that the vertical nature of the list means each priority will just rotate up into the next slot. You may have something you'd like to do that remains No. 6 on the list for four months. A stack-ranked list allows you to continually reevaluate each priority in relation to the others. Clearly, unknown events can and will affect the list, and your ability to RE-prioritize will make the difference between mediocrity and greatness.

When a talented leader takes the time to define priorities, the only projects that get funded and executed are the ones that support the top choices. Harmony and balance are achieved at the company, as it becomes unmistakable what is ego, personal agenda and nonsense, and what is strictly business. Constant Fast is contained, and Revisiting Decisions is squelched.

True prioritization generates revenue in meaningful, productive, and immediate ways. Working from the true priority list offers peace, increased morale, confidence both inside and outside the company, and attends to the first and foremost objective of any organization, which is to maximize profit. Sales floats all boats, as they say, meaning that if you attend to the business of your business, you will be able to accomplish everything else you want to do such as fund employees benefits, support local charities, or even expand into new markets. Without sales, your energy will be concentrated on how to keep the lights on and the payroll running.

When adequate time is given to the strategic decisions made on an annual and quarterly basis, you'll have much more confidence in those decisions because they were made when you were at your best and had time to consider any potential lurking domino effects. You had time for peer review, and projections, sourcing, vendor negotiation and tweaking. But in making ad-hoc, high impact, rushed decisions, you can never be certain there isn't something you've overlooked, necessitating revisiting the decision over and over again.

WHY IT MATTERS

Companies who Exercise Creative Discipline can move to the forefront of their industries because they are simply focusing on the things that truly matter to the business, and the business is allowed to move forward. Nonsense, churn, high turnover due to toxicity, ego and personal agendas get so much of the competition into a turmoil, the company who can think clearly and move forward making sense has an extreme competitive advantage from the get go.

POISON CONTROL

Rate yourself on the following statements, giving yourself a 1 if you rarely do what the statement says, and a 10 if you consistently do what the statement says. If you are brave enough, have your staff rate these statements for your department, then consider the results carefully.

Rate yourself on a scale of 1-10

_____ I have reviewed my department's project dead-lines and processes and found them to adequately reflect the time necessary to complete work at a normal pace.

_____ I hold myself accountable to the same project deadlines and processes as my staff.

_____ I solicit feedback from my staff and from their staff about processes, deadlines, and work pace.

_____ I empower my employees to take their appropriate vacation days.

_____ I take appropriate vacation and rest to recharge my own batteries.

_____ I manage the process of good ideas so that the department's work is focused on the company's strategic goals.

_____ I empower my staff to complete the tactical plan without interference or changes that I might prefer. As long as they deliver results, I am satisfied.

____ I rarely change a project once the resources are committed and the work begun, because I know exactly how it fits into the overall plan for the company.

___ My department operates by a strategic plan that is reviewed quarterly and is updated quarterly as the executive strategic plan is reviewed and tweaked.

____ I can recite the company's goals for the year and for the quarter. Everyone on my team can do the same.

Total your score: _____
The higher the score, the healthier your pond; the lower the score, the more toxic your pond. Make it your goal in the coming months to increase your score on each statement.

Clean Up Method 5: Gain Humility

You are not here merely to make a living. You are here to enable the world to live more amply, with greater vision, and with a finer spirit of hope and achievement. You are here to enrich the world. You impoverish yourself if you forget this errand.

--Woodrow Wilson

Be careful, all who enter here. This chapter contains the most dangerous information in this entire book, though apart from abandoning all hope, you may instead find some. Even so, this chapter is not for the faint of heart. Why? Because the core of the toxic pond problem lies in a place most of us don't ever want to go: into an examination of our motives.

In the wake of Enron's demise, the looting at Tyco, multi-million dollar CEO "severance" packages, and other missteps by senior executives, the spotlight in business has turned back to the character of those individuals leading companies. Apparently, character *does* matter. But is the most critical of all character traits simply lacking in those individuals ruthless enough to make it to the top of organizations? Are the terms "CEO" and "humility" mutually exclusive?

In the process of the examination, it's imperative to ask this question: does responsibility for self-examination increase if an individual becomes responsible for the livelihood of other people? Does responsibility increase *more* as the number of lives impacted increases?

The answer, of course, is a resounding *yes*! Responsibility for self-examination and for ridding one's pond of the worst of all the Seven Deadly Toxins does indeed increase when the individual is responsible for the livelihood of other people. This Toxin is the most sour and despicable of all the Seven Deadly Toxins because of the anguish and heartbreak it perpetuates in the lives of those individuals who are affected by it.

We would all agree the Toxin of Living the Lie should be cleaned up from many different "responsible" categories of workers: ministers, school teachers, priests, nurses, and anyone else with the responsibility of caring for others. Arguably the CEO's and upper level management executives in this country are responsible for the livelihood of *more* individuals than any other single category. When Ford Motor Company closes over a dozen plants and lays off more than 30,000 workers, the Executive Management team has an ethical responsibility to make sure that they've done everything possible to *prevent* that from happening, including looking to see if the Toxin of Living the Lie is present in the pond.

According to an article in the Detroit News, Friday April 06, 2007, new Ford CEO Alan Mulally took home $28 million for his four months of work in 2006. Additional executives took home a total of more than $30 million dollars for their work in 2006, and the packages included such perks as cars, gas cards, cell phones, insurance premium reimbursements, doctor co-pay reimbursements, sports tickets, club memberships, and even the income taxes required by the IRS on all this generosity. Ford Motor Company paid over $58 million dollars to *half a dozen* individuals in the wake of massive lay-offs and plant closures. Even if Mulally is fired, he walks away with another $27.5 million, this time for failure.

Do the decisions to award enormous salaries, bonuses and perks to six individuals have anything to do with to the decisions to close plants and lay off thousands of workers? The decisions are inextricably related through the Toxin of Living the Lie. The duty to manage and govern responsibility is very real and very big. The Clean Up Method of **Gain Humility** is the only way to combat the Toxin of **Living the Lie** and its disastrous fallout. Unfortunately, this clean up is hard to come by. The Clean Up Methods in Part II can be put to work in any company regardless of the leader's character (or lack thereof), as they are task-oriented. *Clean Up Method 5: Gain Humility*, however, is rooted in the heart, not on a checklist. This Clean Up Method is only effective if it is authentic.

THE MISUNDERSTOOD VIRTUE

A virtue is a *morally good quality.* Most people accept that morally good qualities include such things as compassion, discernment, trustworthiness, and integrity. Each of these are qualities that make up a person's character, and the degree to which an individual possesses these qualities is the degree to which we believe them to be good people, and by extension good leaders.

Humility is lauded as something worthy and necessary in many occupations; however, *in business*, it is often felt to be a hindrance to progress. Humility has gotten this bad reputation in the business world because, for some, it promotes weakness. As if the individual who is humble could not possess the inner strength or ambition necessary to drive to a goal, or be strong enough to withstand the stress of the CEO position.

The negative campaign for humility in leadership is built by the arrogant and ego-driven leaders who want nothing to do with it, and don't want the expectation of humility to be any part of their job description. They'll cloak humility in weakness and portray it as a stumbling block to the role of CEO—saying "meekness" causes them to lose effectiveness as a leader. This is all utter nonsense, and a game of words to keep themselves from being accountable to what is worldwide considered to be the foremost virtuous act of humanity: treat others the way you would want to be treated. That is humility.

Embedded in the word itself is a shared root with the Latin humus, which means *dirt* or *earth*. The same Latin root is a part of the word *humanity*. All of humanity shares in the humble origins of creation; none better, none worse. It has been said that death is the great equalizer, fairly treating all to the same outcome: from dust you have come; to dust you shall return. Humility is simply the practical application of that truth. Humility is exercised or not exercised in the way we treat other people. But don't be fooled—humility does not *begin* in the application. The application is merely the evidence of its existence. It bears repeating, because this fact is often lost or confused: *The application is merely the evidence of humility's existence.*

Gaining Humility takes internal reflection and a real desire to be a better *person*, not a better CEO or CMO or other executive position, because a better person makes those offices better. Competence, drive, and even ambition have nothing to do with humility. These qualities can exist in the humblest of CEO's or the most arrogant, because humility is all about how you view and treat others. Humility is a tempering, a balance, preventing ambition from turning into blind ambition, preventing leadership from turning into lordship. Leaders do not possess the virtue of humility when they put their personal agenda above the good of the company's goals, or above the good of the employees' needs. When American Airlines executives distributed millions of dollars among themselves in bonuses and incentive pay, but cut the baggage handlers' wages, were they treating the lowliest of employees the way they would want to be treated? Of course not.

Every person possesses judgment—that ability to make considered decisions. But not every person possesses *good* judgment, because you can't train to it, or manufacture it, or buy it anywhere. Good judgment is intrinsic and deep, a conglomeration of experience, sensibilities, fair play, right and wrong, values and what's best. It's a complex formula, a simultaneous vetting of a situation through the unconscious and the myriad experiences of upbringing and understanding. Good judgement may *grow* in an individual by experiencing situations to which judgment is applied, and that process over time can develop good judgment into wisdom. Leaders hire staff for the work they can do in the business; they should hire executives for the *judgment* they bring to bear on complex situations and problems. But can a CEO who says the three most important things in life are money, power and clout honestly exercise good judgment toward the countless decisions concerning products and customers his company touches? Even if these things are not said out loud, they are established by the CEO's actions. He is a crabapple tree after all.

FROM ILLUSION TO DELUSION

When Ken Lay was arrested for fraud and insider trading, he seemed genuinely surprised. How does an individual get to this point? In his heart of hearts, he never thought what he did was wrong, probably because he also truly believed the rules didn't apply to him. This illustrates the enormous gap between who he is, and who he thinks he is. If you are willing to lie to yourself about yourself, what else will you be willing to do? Caught with his hand in the till, he was still astonished at the handcuffs. Truly, if he had caught someone else with a hand in the till, would his reaction have been the same? Of course not. This disparity is the absence of humility.

Maybe it's the climb up the corporate ladder that helps create this gap. Some leaders begin to believe that the success around them had everything to do with their singular ability. This in combination with heady power, money, and a lifestyle of grandeur, turns the illusion into delusion, and then there is no going back without a fiery crash to the ground. Another CEO without humility, Bernie Ebbers of WorldCom, was sentenced to twenty-five years in prison for his role in the biggest accounting fraud in history. But Bernie's arrogance didn't just cost him his freedom; it cost WorldCom employees their jobs, their livelihoods, and their life's savings.

In a statement from July 22, 2003 to the U.S. Senate Committee on the Judiciary about the WorldCom case, Morton Bahr, President of the Communications Workers of America testified, "More than 22,000 WorldCom employees lost their jobs and thousands more saw their 401(k) retirement savings decimated. Initially, these laid-off WorldCom employees were left with nothing, even as the new WorldCom Board agreed to pay its new CEO $20 million over three years. The AFL-CIO came to the aid of these non-union laid-off WorldCom employees, and won minimal severance benefits of $5,000 each." Bernie Ebbers cried when he was sentenced. Do we think he cried for them?

Sometimes it's not easy to see the absence of humility. The least humble seem to put on a good show of piety now and then, cloaking their avarice and arrogance in spiritual terminology. "Pray for us, we are under siege," is the cry of the CEO whose avarice is on the verge of discovery. One red flag to note is whether the leader has any accountability. Accountability works for all people, from the child who is supposed to feed the dog to the CEO making multi-million dollar decisions about the direction of thousands of lives. A willingness to be accountable demonstrates humility, and transparency demonstrates the greatest humility of all. When a CEO and his executive team have "hidden" their bonuses in strategically categorized paperwork, and stand before the employees, earnestly assuring them they feel their pain because the senior team is also going without bonuses, humility is nonexistent. These leaders have deluded themselves into believing they've exercised good judgment on behalf of the rest of the employees in the room, most of whom live paycheck to paycheck, while they don't even pay for their own gas or taxes. On top of extreme arrogance, a lack of accountability allows this happen.

Unfortunately, the likelihood of arrogant leaders gaining humility is slim. Why? Because, unlike Scrooge, few arrogant executives have the ghosts of the past, present and future to visit them, bringing the aftermath of their selfish motives to life. If something hasn't happened yet in their lives to increase their humility, it's not likely to happen once they have the helm of an enterprise. Corruption starts in the heart, and doesn't necessarily make it any further than that. A leader who prides herself on not stooping to Ken Lay's or Bernie Ebber's crimes may still be developing her own legend and stealing from the employees. Is there any true difference between the CEO who gains money from insider trading, and the CEO who gains money by delaying merit wages for a few weeks to 300 warehouse employees so she can hit her numbers and buy a Mercedes with her bonus? Just because it's legal doesn't make it right.

THE EMPEROR HAS NO CLOTHES

In Hans Christian Anderson's 1837 tale, the Emperor stood before the mirror, naked, surrounded by his advisors, all admiring his non-existent clothes. No one could admit the truth of the situation, because no one wanted to be considered stupid or unfit for their position, trusting the tailors' lie about the special invisible cloth seen only by the wise and intelligent. This fable aptly describes the compensation packages delivered to many corporate leaders today, and the willingness of the "advisors" with whom they surround themselves to support them, i.e. other executives and the Board members who okay these decisions.

Understand that the Toxin of Living the Lie is not in the millions of dollars executives pay themselves, but in the *disparity* between how they treat themselves, and how they treat their employees and customers, which is *most easily displayed* in the disparity in income ratios. In other words, the money is just the most obvious symptom to talk about. According to the latest study by United for a Fair Economy titled "Executives Excess 2007: the Staggering Social Cost of U.S. Business Leadership," the average top executive salary at Fortune 500 companies was a little over $10 million for the year, which equates to over $4,000 per working day in a month. The average worker, at about $30,000 for the year, comes in at about $125 per working day. Is the leader who is being paid that kind of money really that much better at leading than everyone else?

Occasionally a rare leader can come into a situation and make it better for everyone involved. These individuals earn their pay by *increasing the collective good* for everyone. When Alan Questrom took the CEO position at JC Penney in September 2000, the stock price had tumbled to single digits, coming to rest at a dismal $9 per share. Questrom had said that he thought it would take two to five years to turn the giant retailer around, and he was right. When he departed in 2005, the stock price had risen to over $40 per share.

In some cases, the monetary investment may be worthwhile for the entire company—everyone ultimately benefits *including* customers, shareholders and employees. But for the most part, accountability for CEO's and performance doesn't exist. These leaders get their perks completely apart from the measurable objectives, and if they get the boot, they walk away with millions more in severance package agreements. When an executive's gain comes at someone else's loss, the Toxin of Living the Lie needs a clean up.

Recognition of one's own talents and gifts is imperative to move forward and live a fulfilling life. Recognizing oneself to possess extreme talent does not preclude humility. Putting those talents to work for the good of a company and creating success for all is part of being truly humble, because it is recognition of ability without pretense. But hogging the spotlight, taking the attention, preventing others from shining, thinking of one's talents as better than they are, and making financial decisions that benefit executives at the expense of staff all constitute arrogant acts that do not value others as equal to oneself. These things exemplify a complete lack of humility.

Additionally, the hypocrisy is nearly palpable when top executives talk about relating to their employees and customers and live in this disparity. Enormous executive salaries mean rising prices for the customer and lower bonuses and average wages for employees. The way these individual see the world and their customers and their employees is not as equal to, but as better than.

THE NARROWING FUNNEL

Though it has always been morally wrong to be this sort of a jackass, it is becoming increasingly a poor professional decision as well. Business Leadership is accountable in a way they never have been before because information now belongs to the masses. With the Internet and Information

Age explosions, "everyman" is powerful, and has a forum and a voice and an audience. Access to public filings, SEC reports, articles and blogs on corporate responsibility, even sites that allow readers to anonymously blast their terrible boss give a voice to the previously voiceless.

The pressures brought to bear on company leaders are stronger, and the escape routes narrower. Added to this is the passion of the upcoming generations to believe in empowerment, activism, environmentalism and other causes. The stretch for something meaningful in life beyond power and avarice is tightening the noose on the old school ways of doing things.

WHY IT MATTERS

Humility in the workplace matters because people matter. Get close to your employees; know them, learn their names, learn something about them. Understand what life is like for them on their paycheck. Substitute yourself in their jobs for a day or a week, and see how you fare. Treat them with the respect you want to be treated with; these are the individuals who make your position of power possible.

Humility listens, and hears. Leaders who possess humility ask questions and express curiosity. Curiosity implies risk—a risk that something may be uncovered or suggested that the leader didn't already know. What if that something proves the leader wrong in his assessment? What if someone discovers his failure? Ego doesn't risk, but humility does, and greater answers are found with curiosity. Curiosity allows the entire world to be mentor, and humility allows answers and solutions to come from any source. This practice broadens the problem-solving world considerably.

Will the new breed of leaders and managers rise to the challenge and change the world? Well, it's up to you, because you are they. May you take the challenge.

POISON CONTROL

Rate yourself on the following statements, giving yourself a 1 if you rarely do what the statement says, and a 10 if you consistently do what the statement says. If you are brave enough, have your staff rate these statements for your department, then consider the results carefully.

Rate yourself on a scale of 1-10

____ I consistently strive to present myself to my team in a humble manner.

____I consistently listen to my team members and honestly hear what they have to say. I encourage constructive criticism.

___ My boss encourages our team to express our opinions about processes and decisions, and listens well without becoming defensive.

_____ My company has a strong work/life balance ethic.

____ My company leaders do what is right even when no one is looking.

___ I do what is right even when no one is looking.

___ I know the names of my staff and something about their personal lives. I routinely follow up with questions or express concern to them about the issues they are facing.

___ I follow all the same rules that I require from staff, from meeting deadlines to ordering office supplies.

___ I never receive raises and bonuses unless the company is performing so that the staff level workers also receive raises and bonuses.

____ I take time out to self-reflect and compare my motives and behaviors to a higher standard. I try to improve my ethical behavior and strive to practice the Golden Rule.

Total your score: _____
The higher the score, the healthier your pond; the lower the score, the more toxic your pond. Make it your goal in the coming months to increase your score on each statement.

Bonus Offer

*A Special Gift
for
Toxic Clean Up Readers*

**With the purchase of this book, you'll receive a
Bonus Package worth $35—yours FREE.**

Simply visit www.teresaday.com/ToxicCleanUpBonus to receive your free package, which includes:

- Toxic Clean Up Strategy and Action Plan
- Tip Sheet and Plan for empowering employees to make changes at the workplace
- Performance Grid to rate yourself and your workplace on the toxic scale

A $35 value--*free* with the purchase of this book.

Printed in the USA
CPSIA information can be obtained
at www.ICGtesting.com
JSHW082206140824
68134JS00014B/454